Riding the Dream

The Story of

Barbara Jo Rubin

by
DeDe Splaingard

All rights reserved
© 2025 DeDe Splaingard
Justice Mark Ltd
dedesplaingard0205@gmail.com

ISBN 979-8-218-52120-2

First Edition

Publisher and author disclaim all liability of any person alive or dead. All intents and purposes of this story are based on past recollections of events and not intended for misuse, harm, or loss.

DEDICATION

To the angel of Justice

ACKNOWLEGEMENTS

Rose-Bud, Buddha Rose, KeeRo, Kathy Brown, Mary Beer, Terri Lask, Suzy Weis-Osman, Robert Osman, Trudy Boaz, Barb & Edward Houston, Lori & Frank Pace, Sherry Rodemeyer, Penny Boggis, Birgit Spears, Jenn Washington-Riemer, Tara McKay, Mike Richards, Stephanie Grimes, Rochelle Weaver, Dr. Wade White, Therese Rytz, Kathy Kirby, Jane Franke, Julia Schneidewind, Toni & Dean Atchinson, Cathy Sweeney, PJ Cooksey, Carolyn & Larry James, Carolyn & Leroy Hellman, Kim Thorpe-Sampson, Claudia Kaufmann, Don Ellis, Dr. Morgan, Carrie Rule, Carmelo Mendoza, Artemio, Pete Seketa, Joe Brown, Nancy Carver, Randy Grim, Ray Malther, Keith Brauer, Dennis Higgins, Dave Mueller, Fran Natoli, Jim Fraker

SPECIAL CREDITS

Graphic Design – Alexandria Pawlow

Editorial – Kathy Baima

Preface		pg. 7
Introduction		pg. 9
Chapter 1	At the Start	pg. 11
Chapter 2	Rebel with a Cause	pg. 35
Chapter 3	Breaking the Glass Gate	pg. 65
Chapter 4	Riding the Dream	pg. 83
Chapter 5	Fall to Pieces	pg. 107
Chapter 6	Out to Pasture	pg. 117
Chapter 7	Finding Another Path	pg. 129
Chapter 8	Making the Best of It	pg. 145
Chapter 9	Classically Forever	pg. 155

PREFACE

Have you ever heard a captivating story and then wondered about the details beyond statistics, headlines, and facts? Were you intrigued by feelings, circumstances, and the conditions of that time?

I've been told such a story, that is about following a dream that created experiences to fulfill its fate. My fascination in Barbara Jo Rubin's story took me back to the social impact of the pioneer female racehorse jockeys but also included a personal testimony of a life that did not ignore the pure love and understanding of horses.

Enjoy the ride!
DeDe Splaingard

Introduction

Barbara Jo Rubin had a passion, and she owed it to horses. Racehorses, storybook horses, horses you can see in dreams. She was about five years old and remembers the day that changed everything.

Sweet fresh air blew, and the warm Florida sunshine fluttered over her face on the day that her Grandpa Joseph Rubin brought her to a park. This park did not have swings, slides, or picnic tables. Thunder boomed in the distance, and Barbara Jo's forehead crinkled when a young man approached.

Grandpa gave a curt hello and handed over some money. She watched as the stranger squished the bills into his pocket and walked off. Little Barbara Jo wondered, *why is Grandpa giving that man money?*

Grandpa scooped her up into his arms and hurried along a brushy tree line. He stopped at a chain link fence. Overgrown branches tickled her face where they stood quietly. She swatted at the limbs and bramble annoyingly and asked, "Papa, what we *doing?*"

He shushed her. Thunder bellowed and rumbled again, causing the ground to shake. Grandpa made a peek hole in the bramble pointed through the gap.

Barbara Jo saw galloping racehorses with tails flying like kites in the wind. Her wide-eyed stare locked on the colorful jockey silks smearing past her like liquid crayons. The horse hooves pounded the ground, creating the sound of thunder that echoed into the air up to the finish line.

Grandpa's animated shouts and cheers shook her, and she wrapped her arms tight around his neck. She felt his quick pulse as her own little heart pounded.

Going to the park with Grandpa Rubin was a visit to Hialeah Racetrack. Grandpa's eyes pleaded kindly to Barbara Jo and said, "Now, honey, you can just keep this our secret, can't you?"

She nodded, yes.

She did not know that Grandpa was forbidden to gamble anymore. She only knew that being with him at the racetrack made her feel like she was in the presence of something wonderful.

She adored the beautiful horses, the jockeys who looked so gallant and the excitement of the race crowd, especially the roar at the finish line.

She saw magnificence.

She also saw Grandpa's sadness. He referred to the times that he lost bets as bad luck, and he seldom had the good kind. Over time, Barbara Jo realized how some people love horses at the races, and others just love gambling.

Chapter 1

At the Start

*There's something about the outside of a horse
that's good for the inside of a man.*
- Winston Churchill

November 21st, 1949, in the humble county seat hospital of Highland Illinois, Barbara Jo Rubin said hello to the world. On that mild, windy autumn morning, she was an early surprise for her mother, Maxine, and father, Robert. The couple were on a Thanksgiving holiday visit at Maxine's parents in Illinois, miles away from their home in Florida.

Daddy Robert had a hunch that his second child would be another girl and won the bet he made with his buddies.

Their oldest baby daughter, Francine, was a lovable, healthy eighteen-month-old, who was eager for a sibling. Three years later their baby son, Michael, would complete the family.

Robert Rubin was also the only son, too. born to Joseph and Dorothy Rubin. They were first generation Jewish immigrants. His parents, Morris and Becky Ginsberg, fled their Ukrainian homeland in 1898. Morris and his blonde-haired blue-eyed bride raised their children to the universal melting pot of the United States. Morris was an educated man and known for his wanderlust and womanizing personality. Becky was known for her faithful following of Jewish traditions.

They resided permanently in Brooklyn where their youngest daughter, Dorothy, was born in 1901, wed Joseph Rubin and had two children, Alma and Robert.

Dorothy rode out difficult times when her husband's penchant for horse race gambling cost him the livelihood of his Triborough Coach Company in Brooklyn. Leaving behind a life of bankruptcy, the family moved to Florida for a clean start. However, Grandpa Joseph would forever be a horseracing gambler.

The state of Florida held the ever-sunny dream of prosperity, especially the opulence of the south Miami area that was coined as the American Riviera in the 1950's. South Miami was a destination that many flocked to for its beauty and opportunities. Growing up, Barbara Jo Rubin lived most notably in Opa Locke, Florida. Her paternal grandparents, Joseph and Dorothy Rubin lived nearby in Miami within a seventy-five-mile radius of three prominent horse racing tracks.

Opa Locke was due north of Miami with a population of 5,000 during this time. Opa Locka was originally known as, Opa-tisha-wocka-locka, by the Native American Seminole tribe, meaning big island covered with many trees and swamps.

During the 1950's, creating the American dream was not as difficult as eluding the widespread viral epidemic of polio.

The disease did not discriminate, and contracting polio was all too common before the widely accredited Salk vaccine.

Barbara Jo was one of the statistics who awoke one morning, unable to move her legs. Maxine rushed her daughter to the family physician fearing the inevitable.

When the office exam potentially indicated polio, Barbara Jo was admitted to Children's Variety Hospital in Hialeah, where a painful spinal tap positively diagnosed poliomyelitis. The viral infection attacked her lower thoracic nerves down the spinal cord to her legs, unlike cases that assaulted the respiratory system that required treatment with the iron lung ventilator.

Polio patients were quarantined to prevent the contagious viral spread. Little Barbara Jo was kept in the hospital bedridden with both feet laced into shoes attached to the wall. The continual tension pulled her legs taunt to prevent muscle atrophy and potential paralysis. A few times a day the hospital staff unlaced her legs to relieve the traction. This was painful.

"You can pinch me when it hurts", the nurse said to Barbara Jo while a physical therapist massaged the fibrous flesh behind her knees. Barbara Jo pinched the nurse hard and cried out from burning painful muscle spasms.

Barbara Jo often saw those who were in a metal capsule with only their heads exposed. The iron lung was a life sustaining measure but looked like a science fiction nightmare to a child. Any length of solitary confinement could make a child sullen and bored, but Barbara Jo remembers amusing herself with a vivid imagination.

She thought about her very favorite thing in the world - horses. To her, horses seemed like large people with fascinating eyes and were playful friends that she made up stories and scenarios about.

Her imaginary world with horses kept her company, in the hospital just like at home where she had a collection of ceramic and glass horse figurines. Each pony in her home menagerie was given a name, and she bid them hello at the start of the day calling out, *good morning, Furioso, good morning, Trigger, good morning, Black Beauty.*

The Children's Variety Hospital was bustling with commotion and treatments. At night she rested. She dreamt of riding a pearly white pony in a lush meadow. The pony's hooves pounded a staccato rhythmic beat of duh-dum, duh-dum, duh-dum. The pony snorted triumphantly. Barbara Jo's wide smile formed soft creases around her sapphire eyes.

As a child, Barbara Jo's favorite movie was National Velvet. The story's heroine, Velvet (played by a young starlet, Elizabeth Taylor) wins a horse in a raffle, named Piebald (The Pie).

Velvet trains Pie for high level eventing and enters the Grand National Steeplechase race, but she is not allowed to ride in the race because she is a girl; Velvet went undercover dressed as a boy to ride The Pie and win.

The 1944 film captured an enduring bond between a girl and her horse. During the making of the movie art imitated life. Fourteen-year-old Elizabeth Taylor had such chemistry with King Charles (the horse portraying The Pie) that he was given to Taylor who kept King Charles for the rest of his life.

Children find their own reasons to love horses, whether having or ever meeting a real one. Boys might relate to cowboy ruggedness, and little girls might gush at their splendor. Horse passion is not gender specific and is timelessly historic.

The classic children's book, Black Beauty, written by Anna Sewell in 1877, is narrated from a horse's point of view. It tells sentimental emotions of Beauty's life with all its glory and pain from his birthplace on a quiet farm to his life as a working horse in bustling 19th century England.

Sewell wrote her bestseller later in her career after being crippled by an injured ankle. Disabled, Sewell used horse-drawn carriages for mobility which contributed to her devoted respect for horses and concern for their humane treatment.

The colonial settlers brought the European sport of kings, known as horse racing, to America. Decades later in the early 1950's, technology brought televised horse racing into America's living rooms.

The 1953 Gotham Stakes race made a national hero of the horse, Native Dancer. He was nicknamed the Grey Ghost, for his speed and the haunting appearance of his grey coat on black and white television sets.

Horses were prominent in television shows of the era. Audiences avidly tuned in to watch The Lone Ranger, Roy Rogers and Trigger, My Friend Flicka and Mr. Ed, making horses both entertainment and sports icons for this early mass media American culture.

The horse is an essential part of human civilization; a partner that drove Roman chariots, carried hunters, warriors and explorers upon their backs. Horses were enlisted in wars on battlefields. Teams of horses plowed farms, hauled timber, and worked in coal mines. The mail was delivered via pony express. Horses were personal and public transportation before the automobile. The good book of all times, the Bible, refers to the horse multiple times.

Language has become peppered with equine references. Success can be signified with the statement, "hit your stride" and when forced to quit a job or retire, it is said that we are "put out to pasture." Horsepower signifies a unit of power equal to 550 foot-pounds per second.

And to some, horses were just good medicine.

When it came time for their little girl to be released from the hospital after fighting polio, Dr. Cantor told Maxine and Bob Rubin that Barbara Jo's prognosis was good but that her leg development was compromised. Dr. Cantor emphasized that

Barbara Jo would need a leg strengthening regimen and recommended swimming.

Before going home, Barbara Jo suited up for a swim in the hospital pool. The muscles behind her knees were weak, and it was difficult to straighten her legs. She didn't take to swimming. She wasn't strong enough to keep herself afloat and sank like a rock. Dr. Cantor suggested another choice, horseback riding. And in that moment, Barbara Jo considered polio a blessing because it meant that she would need to ride horses.

Barbara Jo still declares, "I always knew that horses would be a part of my life forever".

It is not unprecedented for horseback riding to aid or remedy human physical impairment. The thirty second president of the United States of America, Franklin Delano Roosevelt, was diagnosed with polio later in life at age thirty-nine and was an advocate of equine therapy.

Mr. Roosevelt eventually needed to use a wheelchair, but he benefitted from riding horses and spoke highly about horse riding with Prime Minister Winston Churchill. The conversation inspired Churchill's famous statement, *there's something about the outside of a horse that's good for the inside of a man*.

An equine companionship specifically good for a woman resulted in Olympic history. Danish dressage equestrian, Lis Hartel contracted polio at twenty-three years old. She was also pregnant. Lis delivered a healthy baby girl but was left paralyzed.

Three years of intensive physical therapy restored use of her arms and enough partial leg movement to continue dressage. Hartel placed second in the highest level of the Scandinavian riding championships but could not participate in Denmark's Olympic dressage team due to a forty-year aristocratic rule that only permitted commissioned military officers the honor of Olympic level dressage competition and restricted civilians from the event.

The Olympic committee, on its own resolve, banished the elitist restriction for the 1952 Helsinki Olympic Games. Hartel was then chosen to represent Denmark. Paralyzed from the knees down, she was assisted on and off her horse for the events and won two silver medals.

Beyond Olympian medals, Lis Hartel has stated that her most important lifetime achievements were opening the Therapeutic Riding Center of Europe and being a spokesperson for the Polio Foundation.

For her daughter's rehabilitation, Maxine Rubin put Barbara Jo in horseback riding classes locally at Greynolds Park. The group equitation lessons cost three dollars an hour and were instructed by an Army veteran horseman. The expense was a stretch for the family budget, but the benefits quickly outweighed financial woes.

Barbara Jo's body became stronger, and her legs gained strength from posting up and down in the stirrups. The rhythm and sensation of the horse's body stimulated her muscles, her nerve endings, and her heart. Barbara Jo's therapeutic connection to horseback riding built her endurance too, and she cleaned stalls and tack to earn an additional lessons.

Barbara Jo felt, "(that) it wasn't like work for me. It was wonderful just to stay around the horses."

The weekly riding classes enriched her to a skill level fit for entering her first horse show at age seven. The Greynolds Park annual student horse show was a big competition, and Barbara Jo rode a student horse in the show named Spooky. They were performing fine in the outdoor arena until a peacock flew out of a tree.

Spooky, (lived up to his name) spooked, dropping Barbara Jo off his back right in front of the judges. One judge apprehensively questioned the child, "Would you like to continue?"

"Sure". Barbara Jo answered without hesitation and re-mounted. The audience applauded her dedication to finish the show class. Ribbons are not given to riders who come off their horse during a show, so Barbara Jo left empty handed. However, she had already won personal rewards from horseback riding; freedom from polio afflictions and unfortunately, the distraction from a deteriorating home life.

It's hard for a little girl to understand abuse. Inside the walls of their home, her father's raging temper, gambling, drinking, and wayward ways created domestic dysfunction. As a means of diversion, Barbara Jo found sanctuary with horses, whether she was working around them or riding.

In the horse world, equines don't tolerate abuse from each other. Horses follow a moral code of primal ethics that nature devises. Humans make choices.

Shamanic belief professes that kinship to a horse provides strength and that the horse spirit is healing to those connected to it, especially in times of difficulty.

As a grade schooler Barbara Jo was aware of her dad's long and random absence from home and noticed that nobody cried when he was gone.

Mother Maxine, worked at the store that Grandma Dorothy Rubin ran to close the financial gap of her wanderlust husband. During summer school vacations, Maxine took the kids to stay at their grandparents' farm, in Illinois. Barbara Jo recalls this being a fun time every year.

The Wehrle farm was in the township of Mulberry Grove fifty-two miles east of St. Louis, Missouri. Packed for travel, Maxine and the kids drove to their annual summer oasis in late May, usually over the Memorial Day holiday weekend. It was a two-day road trip of adventure driving from Florida to the farm.

The Illinois rural roads were like driving back in time. Maxine appreciated the pace of her childhood hometown. Life in Mulberry Grove (population 500) was simpler to her, not easier, just more authentic.

During WWII, nineteen-year-old Maxine left home for the first time to go to California as part of the national wartime workforce effort of the patriot icon, Rosie the Riveter. While in San Diego, Maxine met a marine, Robert Rubin, who was stationed near the machine shop where she worked. The rest is history, as they say; Maxine's history of doing her best in life decisions.

The Wehrle's were hard working Baptist farm people. Grandma Nina grew a bountiful garden of vegetables, sewed summer clothes for the girls, and helped Michael read. Grandpa Clarence owned and ran the local grain elevator and tended to his own livestock.

There were chickens, pigs, and cows to care for and a plethora of household chores at the farm. Grandma did laundry the old-fashioned way, using one sudsy tub of lye soap and water to hand wash the clothes and then another tub of clean water to rinse them out. Nina used a hand ringer to push the excess water from the clothing. The kids hung the wash outside on the clothesline to dry which made the household linens and clothing smell like sunshine.

The youngsters were given structure and responsibility at Grandma and Grandpa's along with a fair share of childhood adventures. To a kid, it was a Norman Rockwellian life.

On summer evenings the Wehrle's took their grandchildren to local county fairs. Clarence was fond of watching the horse harness races. He was raised with horses by his father, who ran a livery stable in St. Louis, Missouri. Teenage Clarence courted his one-and-only girl, Nina, by driving a horse and buggy out for dates.

Clarence shared his love of horses with his grandchildren, giving them a pony for fun at his farm. The Rubin kids named the black and white paint mare, Sherry. Sherry was a tall pony at fourteen hands and a farm pet for them all, but it was Barbara Jo who would ride bareback non-stop for hours.

Barbara Jo's brother, Mike, would yell into the house, "My turn to ride! Gramma Nina, Barbara won't lemme have my turn".

Older sister Francine would often pass for her turn on Sherry as she found other interests more appealing. Barbara Jo shared riding Sherry with Michael, but it became obvious to Clarence for the farm to have more horses.

Sherry was bred yearly, bringing a foal one by one to the Wehrle herd. Babies added the education of starting up young foals and caring for the entire equine lifespan.

Grandpa Clarence was a lovable man with a dry humor and full of vitality. He was small-framed and kept very fit and healthy. He rarely expressed anger. In the rare instances that it was necessary to discipline, he used a hickory switch.

When Grandpa called out, "Barbara, you're gonna get a whipping for that", she understood her consequences. He was fair with his authority in the way that a child could understand and learn to respect.

Grandma Nina was just as honorable and vibrant. Her sandy brown hair was neatly kept, and she wore calico cotton dresses for everyday chores. She was an avid seamstress and a fabulous cook whose forte was big desserts. Nina's Sunday dinner was always fried chicken. She'd do the dirty work of chopping off the chicken's head but had the grandkids chase and bring the headless bird to the kitchen.

Barbara Jo spent summer free time endlessly bareback riding Sherry which made her strong enough to also climb trees, chop wood, and drive tractors. She was the epitome of a happy go-lucky farm tomboy whose summers went by too fast in Illinois.

Back home in Florida during the rest of the school year, Barbara Jo was shy. Her introvert personality was tested by her Aunt Alma, who owned a clothing boutique. Alma recruited Barbara Jo to model children's outfits from her store at the luxurious Bal Moral Hotel.

Alma's models mingled and played among the hotel guests at the hotel swimming pool. Moms wore cat eye sunglasses relaxing in chaise lounge chairs next to their husbands in Bermuda swim shorts. The adults sipped fruity cocktails smiling at their freckling fair skin kids swimming in the lovely poolside haven amid a beautiful garden with flocks of flamingos.

Patrons happily spent their disposable income on poolside purchases resulting in successful sales. Family guardians attended and supervised their models enjoying the amenities of

The Bal Moral Hotel, too. It was a case of the more the merrier and all kinds of fun in the sun.

Grandma Dorothy watched Barbara Jo, and often say proudly to Grandpa Joseph, "Oh, look how cute, Itsy-Bitsy looks!"

Itsy-Bitsy was their affectionate nickname for their petite granddaughter who was like the spider in the children's song, with spindly legs. If she had to be called by a nickname, Barbara Jo always preferred itsy-bitsy over pee wee.

Barbara Jo could care less about fashion apparel but by participating at the shindig she learned to overcome shyness and be comfortable around groups of people.

Sister Francine enjoyed these galas and years later became a model, dancer and beauty pageant contestant. Barbara Jo had the most fun at the pool parties playing with the Gubin kids that were family friends who were also participants in Alma's pool side affairs.

The Gubin family was Jewish and came from Indiana to Miami Beach in 1953. Harold and Ruth fell in love with Florida after a family vacation with their five children. Their youngster, Gordon, a year older than Barbara Jo, tagged around as Barbara Jo's escort at the Bal Moral Hotel poolside. Folks called him Gordie.

He was an energetic and sweet boy with thick, curly dark hair and intense hazel eyes. Harold and Ruth Gubin were Jewish and ran a deli in Sunny Isles Beach called, Gubie's Deli. Their market was one of many gathering spots for the large Florida Jewish community. The popularity of Jewish delis on Miami Beach began when post WWII generations, largely from New York City took residency in the area. The waves of the east coast crowd regarded Miami Beach as New York with sand.

Barbara Jo's dad, (Robert) Bob, was once a Velda Farms Dairy delivery man for Gubie's Deli where he befriended the Gubin family which led to a lifelong bond. Some folks even mistook them as relatives, confusing the similarity of their surnames, Rubin/Gubin.

Prior to becoming a delivery man, Bob had a short-lived career as a motorcycle cop before being fired for his hot-headedness. It was an understatement that Bob had a disdain for rules and regulations and would fall far and often from conventional jobs. By grade school age, Barbara Jo saw her dad in many questionable business matters. One wintery night, she woke up thirsty after bedtime and shuffled down the hallway toward the kitchen for a drink and found her dad gathered with men in the kitchen and knew that she would be in trouble if caught awake, so she planned to sneak past the kitchen through the hall to the bathroom for a drink and get back to bed unnoticed.

The men were intent on a metal box (a safe) in the middle of the kitchen terrazzo floor as her dad used a blow torch on it. Bob was determined to crack open the safe and happened to glance up to see his daughter watching wide-eyed.

"What the hell are you doing awake?" he growled.

The rest of the men gawked over at the frozen pixie in her nightgown.

"MAXINE" Bob roared, "Come get this kid outta here!"

The household awoke, but only Maxine went out into the kitchen. The tone of Bob's voice meant only one thing; someone was going to get a beating.

Maxine saw what was happening and directed, "Barbara Jo, get back into bed".

While Barbara Jo scooted past her mom she tried to explain, "But Mom, I was just getting a drink ..."

Maxine watched the men scattering around her house in an uproar. She consoled her three scared children by calling them in the bedroom, "Now, you all go back to sleep now, okay".

The commotion of cracking a safe quickly concluded and after the men left her house, Maxine was punished. The kids stayed in the bedroom that night but got a share of abuse from hearing it happen to their mom. Bob was especially angry since the contents of the stolen safe only held a few dollars.

Often alcoholics have the idea of earning a living by running a bar. For Bob Rubin's first attempt as a bar keeper, he ran The Kentuckian located in North Miami.

On weekdays, The Kentuckian's working folk crowd bought Maxine's prepared home cooked roast beef sandwiches and deviled eggs with their libations. On the weekends, Bob ran poker games upstairs in a room that was only accessible from a ladder. Maxine found herself with kids in tow, trying to keep up a legitimate business front while Bob drank and gambled away revenue. The Kentuckian soon closed due to rumors that the joint was too hot for gamblers.

Next, Bob opened a night club funded with the cash and the namesake from retired boxing world light-heavyweight champ, Joey Maxim. The club, Joey Maxim's Voo Doo Room, was located behind Miami-Dade County's historic Greynolds Park and was a reasonable success.

The handsome Golden Age Italian boxer, Giuseppe Antonio Berardinelli took his ring name from the maxim automatic machine gun. Joey was welcomed around the family and Barbara Jo remembers Joey as a big cuddly teddy bear and a very kind man.

One summer at the Wehrle farm, a line was drawn between Clarence Wehrle and his son-in-law. Bob and Joey drove to the farm to deliver a beautiful new Cadillac that Grandpa bought from Bob.

Quite quickly, federal agents caught wind of the car sale and seized the Cadillac as stolen property. Clarence was put on the spot for details of the purchase and probed his son-in-law for legitimacy. Bob warned Clarence to keep his mouth shut. Clarence realized the audacity of Bob's character and forbid Bob to set foot on his property ever again.

In yet, another business venture Bob ran a filling station along a popular intersection of town. To cheat more profit, Bob swapped out the higher-grade fuel tanks with the cheaper gasoline by siphoning the vats at night while Maxine and the kids acted as lookouts from the car.

The best thing about the gas station was how it featured pony rides on the lot, and that was exciting for Barbara Jo. She cared for the ponies and single-handedly trained one little mare named Star to lie down and bow.

Bob's gas station closed after six months, forcing him to sell off the ponies, but Barbara Jo convinced her dad to keep Star. She now had her own pony! (but needed a place to keep her).

Nearby Opa Locka was a large horse ranch named Spooky Acres. The public boarding facility was on the grounds of an old dairy farm. Despite its uncanny name, Spooky Acres was a wonderland. There were over one hundred and fifty horses; riding rings, cowboys and cowgirls all with access to large, wide-open pastures. Star boarded at Spooky Acres and Barbara Jo became a resident, too.

Spooky Acres gave Barbara Jo a sense of community. Her friends were no longer imaginary horse figurines on her bedroom shelf or only for the summer at Grandpa's farm. Barbara Jo rode her little black mare, Star, bareback everywhere on the property. She also made friendships with other like-minded horse people.

With her mother's permission, Barbara Jo packed a sleeping bag and often stayed weekends at Spooky Acres in an empty cow manger. Maxine brought her daughter food and clean clothes in the mornings and forced her to come home on Sunday night.

Surprises and adventures always awaited at Spooky Acres. On a sunny spring morning Barbara Jo found a newly born gray filly in the stall with Mama Star. The pair were healthy and fine and gave Barbara Jo more to take care of, which was fine with her.

During that time, friends from Spooky Acres took Barbara Jo along to prospect horses for sale and made a stop at a pony ride establishment. The ponies waited along a hitching line saddled up for riders.

Barbara Jo was attracted to a beautiful chocolate colt with a flaxen (platinum blonde) mane and tail. The pony had a white blaze that stretched down between his nostrils and eyes that sparkled with a mischievous look. Barbara Jo fell in love.

Customers approached and bought pony ride tickets for their kids. Barbara Jo begged her friends to stay a little longer to watch the pony named Shorty, in action.

The pony ride ring was operated like a miniature racetrack and relied on equine good behavior to thrill young riders. Kids were buckled into the saddle and rode unassisted while the trained ponies trotted gently inside the arena ring for three laps, like a live merry-go-round. Shorty and rider were led by the proprietor as the last to enter the pen before being released from the lead rope.

Shorty took off like a bat out of hell, bolting past the other ponies, biting at them as he ran his three laps at full gallop. The little girl held on while screaming at the top of her lungs.

After his allotted three laps, Shorty exited the ring and went back to the hitching area. The upset parents grabbed their children and quickly drove off.

Barbara Jo followed the owner, who took Shorty out behind a small hay shed. When he started beating Shorty in the head with his fists, she spoke up.

"Stop! Listen, Sir, I've got a great pony to trade for you. My pony is much more suitable for kids, plus I'll give you her filly, too. What do you say?"

"I can't do nothin' with this ornery beast. Don't know why you'd want him. Yeah, let's make a deal."

Shorty wasn't an easy project for the pubescent owner. On his last runaway ride, Barbara Jo reached around his head and cupped her hands over his nostrils and got his attention. Barbara Jo kept his attention from then on and trained Shorty for western barrel racing and jumping.

Growing up, Barbara Jo kept healthy and fit except for a spontaneous case of appendicitis. She came out of the anesthesia, remembering a dreamy hallucination where she saw herself in the old days of the Wild West as Calamity Jane.

Shorty and Barbara Jo

Born in 1852 as Martha Jane Canary, Calamity Jane was a legendary American frontier woman. Jane was a devoted friend of Wild Bill Hickok, a folk legend associated with gun fighting and gambling) and she dressed in menswear to better fit her tough natured, whiskey drinking spirit. Portrayed in the 2004 HBO, Deadwood series, Calamity Jane's noteworthy traits were unconventional. Barbara Jo would grow into a woman of more feminine charm and sober personality than her dreamy counterpart but fearless and unconventional just the same. Barbara Jo admired how her sister, Francine, cornered the market on beauty and feminine genteel. They grew up sharing a bedroom where Barbara Jo's part of the room was all horses and rugged rodeo motifs. Francine's side of the bedroom was softer suited, painted in pink and decorated with ballerina figures, dancers and fashion posters.

The contrasting personalities never caused animosity to their sisterhood. Francine and Barbara Jo were good friends, respected each other's differences and truthfully - both shared the family beauty.

All the Rubin kids learned at an early age to respect differences by necessity. They witnessed the canyon-sized contradictions between their mom and dad. Bob wasn't much of a good father. Maxine was a tender mother who held the family together and raised the children through home life with an alcoholic renegade, always giving them unquestionable love.

The kids each wondered why their mom stayed with their dad. Maxine chose her bad marriage for the sake of the family. Decades later, after the children were raised, the couple divorced. Bob took a younger wife. Maxine never re-married. Maxine was always the responsible head of the household and was an example to her friend, Ruth Gubin, who followed step.

Ruth Gubin was widowed after a thirty-year marriage. Alone, she finished raising her five children. Ruth worked at the Deauville Hotel for endless hours. Ruth and Maxine swapped caring for each other's brood among a busy domestic schedule. The Gubin and Rubin kids grew up similarly through hardships although caused by different circumstances.

Horses live naturally in the social hierarchy of a herd. The herd provides a community of care and survival. Appropriate leadership communicates instinctively the needs of the individual to the others. Animal behaviorists call this focal communication. Focal communication concludes that horses can read intent. Herd animal survival succeeds by communicating honestly through behavior to one another. Horses don't lie.

To understand a horse, one needs to interpret the horse's way of reasoning. A human/horse relationship needs trust to be its best in companionship, work or sport.

You can't do that well, as an outsider.

Barbara Jo stepped into the herd to understand. The more she understood, the more the horses would tell her.

Chapter 2

Rebel with a Cause

Well behaved women seldom make history.
– Laurel Thatcher Ulrich

The early 1960's started the Age of Aquarius, of a cultural landscape shaping into a future of possibilities or problems depending on one's opinion of the changes. The notions of evolution and revolution pulsed through the country's veins.

Adolescence is a time of change that can shift a person's beliefs and dreams but for Barbara Jo these years were filled exploring her adventurous spirit and horses remained deeply important to her.

Horsemen hint to their calling as just being in their blood. Barbara Jo shared a bloodline to horses from Grandpa Wehrle, who valued the sense of a horse and with Grandfather Rubin who valued the cents of horse racing.

At Spooky Acres Barbara Jo shared the horse passion with a good friend, Wendy Warman. Wendy had an older brother who ran horse match races along the outskirts of town at old ranches, an abandoned air strip, or empty fields. The clandestine races went off randomly, and details were spread through the grapevine word of mouth.

The girls dug up intel about the races like archeologists. When they watched a match for the first time, they hid among the rowdy patrons that cheered for their favorite stake. The illegal two-horse head-to-head races were spectacles of wagering, drinking, and fighting. No place for girls.

Match races had a reputation for triumph or tragedy, and authorized racetracks seldom held them. The notorious 1938 challenge match between War Admiral and Seabiscuit earned Seabiscuit claim to fame. But in 1975, the ill-fated mare, Ruffian, broke down live on television against Foolish Pleasure.

Mr. match-race, Dick Warman was a rugged twenty-two-year-old married guy who swaggered like an outlaw. He rode a gorgeous chestnut quarter horse and was a good horseman. Warman got things done his way for his reasons.

Tweenager Barbara Jo spoke to the dude himself, "Lemme race for you."

He sized up petite Barbara Jo, shrugged his shoulders and agreed. Age or gender didn't matter to him. Warman calculated how her eighty-pound body weight could better the chances of his horses. Warman questioned her skills and had Barbara Jo try out first.

In a nearby pasture, Dick brought his horse, his tack and a competitor, another girl, named Jackie. Rubin brought her courage.

Warman saddled up an ebony horse for Barbara mentioning, "This fellow will jump like a jack rabbit at the start for the lead."

She admired the sleek black steed that resembled racehorses she saw on tv. The horses pranced side by side behind the hand drawn line in the dirt bouncing the riders in anticipation.

The quiet afternoon turned into a drag race with Warman's holler out, "Alright, Ready? Let's see what you can do!"

Warman dropped his arm down and the race started. Barbara Jo's horse sprung forward first with the lead. Then she heard the girth snap and felt the saddle moving loose beneath her. Jackie and the other horse took the lead.

Barbara Jo grabbed a handful of thick black mane for balance, pulled her feet out of the stirrups and let the saddle fly off. She caught up and passed the competitor to win the race; riding bareback.

Barbara Jo trotted back over to Warman. With a broad grin, he said, "Oh shit, girl, you can ride".

Barbara Jo mastered racing for Dick Warman and won many, many match races. Warman rewarded her victories with ice cream cones saying, "Here, kid". Occasionally adding, "You did alright".

Barbara Jo didn't get paid and didn't get hurt riding Warman's match races. The experience developed the image to be a professional jockey for her, like a Polaroid picture coming to life. Once again, her exposure to horse racing was kept secret. This time because she was so young and the races were illegal.

Girls in junior high school wore fashionable and stylish tennis shoes. Barbara Jo sported hard orthopedic oxford shoes due to the childhood polio. She appeared to her classmates as a string bean plain-Jane in her own world. She hated junior high and schoolwork, and that showed in her grades and often resulted in academic detention.

Barbara Jo's brother, Michael, was her best buddy. They fished, hunted, and did hard work together. He was an ethical young man who rode horses but preferred to ride motorcycles more. His motorcycle interest grew from idolizing their dad when he was a Miami motorcycle police officer. Mike's love for steel horses lasted far longer than Bob's law enforcement career. Bob was fired for anger management issues.

Mike was a kind and social boy who treated his sisters as equals. Francine was the most outgoing sibling, who joined cheerleading and baton squad while Barbara Jo kept more to herself grooming her natural athletic abilities.

In high school, she had a casual friendship with classmate, Tommy Toms. They hunted and shot rifles with just a hint of rivalry. Competing against men foreshadowed her future, but not before she competed against a half ton rodeo bull. This came about in the nearby town of Davie.

Davie was a nostalgic themed Ol' Wild West town, geared for tourists. Main street was lined with hitching posts for horse parking that the ranch hands used after working cattle ranches.

The town offered professional rodeo events, gun shops, and western apparel stores. Barbara Jo was interested in the bull riding in Davie; not as a spectator, but as a rider.

During a riding practice she sat behind the bull shoot in the event arena watching a young Brahma bull toss off cowboys quickly. She leaned over the ring rail and asked the rodeo staff for a try. They laughed at her. This bull wasn't an easy ride for anyone, much less a novice. She wore them down with her persistence and sweet smile.

The cowboys fixed her rig in the chute and patted down the wrap on her hand. Her adrenaline pumped as the gate flung open. The bull pitched her back and forth with spastic momentum.

She stayed on the bull, and the cowboys smirked at her beginner's luck. They dared her to try again, and she accepted their challenge.

This time, after the guys loaded the same bull, put Barbara Jo on its back, they "jack-assed" a prank. When the gate opened, they jammed a broom in the bull's butt.

The irate bull didn't buck. Instead, he ran full speed to the end of the arena, stopped on a dime, and propelled Barbara Jo over his head. Then the bull thrashed and tossed her like a rag doll because her hand was caught in the rigging.

The staff acted fast to rescue her. When she dropped to the ground the bull gored her in the back. The cowboys used their quarter horses to make a protective shield between Barbara Jo and the bull to get her out of the ring.

Barbara Jo brushed herself off like it was no big deal and went home. When her mom saw the injuries, it was a big deal.

Maxine scolded Barbara Jo for her reckless behavior and made Barbara Jo vow to stay away from the danger of bull riding. If only Maxine could have warned her daughter about the danger of Ronnie Blardinelli.

Blardinelli was an upper classman from a neighboring high school who rode horses at Spooky Acres. He was a 6'5" tall handsome Italian boy with dimples and brown eyes. Ronnie noticed Barbara Jo around the ranch, making a point to get to know her.

Barbara Jo thought Blardinelli was a good rider and that his big brown eyes reminded her of a gentle calf. As they got better acquainted, a mutual interest took shape. Ronnie took Barbara Jo to rodeos, movies, horse auctions and horse shows. He was her first boyfriend.

The fella knew of Bob Rubin's mean reputation and was punctual to pick up his daughter, but it was always Maxine who would answer the door and impose a strict curfew.

During a nice long trail ride together, Barbara Jo shared her dream to become a racehorse jockey with her boyfriend. She expressed her passion and the feeling that she was good at it.

Blardinelli scowled and laughed. Barbara Jo hid the disappointment in his reaction but couldn't forget it.

Bob Rubin moved the family out of Opa Locka to a residence called Country Club Ranches, in the town of Miramar in nearby Broward County. He had bought seven and a half acres with gung-ho plans to build a large barn, fence off the property and build a house. The family was excited about the idea he created. The barn went up first with a one-room apartment attached for family living quarters until building the house. Barbara Jo and Michael worked alongside Bob chopping down pine trees in the lots, stripping the timbers into logs for fence posts and rails. It was laborious and back-breaking work, but it felt good to build something together.

At Country Club Ranches, the Rubins boarded horses for a steady source of income. Barbara Jo took on the work at the barn and loved it. She made her own portion of earnings by privately training the boarders' horses.

Noteworthy horse trainers recognize a horse's natural capabilities and are insightful to the horse's potential to learn. A matrix of horse training talent was quickly growing in Barbara Jo. She had no teacher or mentor. She just listened to what she heard from the horses.

The safety Barbara Jo felt around horses created serenity within her. Her mornings would start with the roar of euphoric whinnies. The horses' keen senses heard and smelled her approaching, and their rumbling high-pitched neighs stirred the dawn with excitement. The barn aromas of oats, manure, saddle soap, hay and leather tack were a mystical incense to the horse aficionado. She never took for granted how much she loved the very sight of horses and Barbara Jo joyously laughed out loud watching them turned out in the pastures, where they playfully chased each other bucking and kicking their muscular bodies high in the air with the agility of a prima ballerina, then landing on the ground with the thud of a sumo wrestler. They rolled on the ground groaning in exertion to flip over before standing up to shake off swirling dots of dust or mud like a Pollock painting. As the horses grazed, their lips made soft tugging sounds on the grass that serenaded her.

Extra-curricular time became a precious commodity in Barbara Jo's life between taking care of horses and schoolwork. There was little room for dating and her feelings for Blardinelli waned. Barbara Jo decided it best to break up and telephoned the boyfriend, who took the news amicably at the time.

Within a few days, Blardinelli asked Barbara Jo to meet and talk. They took a drive along the quiet, desolate roads out past the canals and swamps where he pulled the truck over and stopped to propose.

Barbara Jo listened to his manifesto and then kindly answered, "No, that's not what I want. I need to break up with you".

He moved closer to Barbara Jo, "I just want you back."

Blardinelli did not accept no, and a juvenile delinquency came over him to take what he couldn't have. He aggressively wedged Barbara Jo's head beneath the truck's passenger door armrest and pinned down her arms. He laid on top her and showed predatory precision.

"Ronnie, get off me", she trembled.

All that happened was against her will. She felt the vulgar pain as he raped her. She no longer thought that he had the gentle eyes of a calf.

He opened the truck door and shoved her out onto the rock road. She bolted off the ground and screamed as he drove away, "How could you!? My Dad is gonna kill you for this!"

Not an idle threat. Bob Rubin was completely capable of such a thing. Barbara Jo ran home crying but at the front door, she dried her tears and recanted the courage to tell anyone what happened. It's said that you lose your virginity but hers had been stolen.

If Maxine knew what had happened to her daughter, justice would have been served. Maxine despised stealing; gambling stole her household finances; alcohol stole her marriage. Her strength beneath her tenderness was fierce.

Adult female horses are called mares. They can be quite territorial over self and brood. The queen bee of mares is the boss mare who reigns over the herd in partnership with the stallion. Boss mares lead the herd, providing the way to the necessities of food, water and shelter. The stallion follows behind his herd to protect against lurking predators.

Both the (sire) stallion DNA and the mare bloodline are essential in horse breeding, but it is the mares' daily nurture that is most vital in the baby's development.

Horses were Barbara Jo's compass to her destiny and how she navigated herself. At this juncture in life, Barbara Jo shut down to wanting anything else.

"So, have you seen Barbara Jo lately?"

Eighteen-year-old Gordie Gubin was the Deauville Hotel parking valet when Newt Hofstader (Barbara Jo's uncle) asked the out-of-the-blue question. Gordie hadn't set sight on Barbara Jo for years, but quickly remembered that even as a kid, how her sapphire eyes were unforgettable.

Newt purred with a Cheshire cat grin and answered, "Oh, she's beautiful... just *beautiful*." Gordie decided to pay the Rubin's an overdue visit.

Bob answered the door and was quite happy to see Gordie. They shook hands and sat together in the kitchen reminiscing about the families and mentioning how much they both missed Harold, Gordie's father. While they were talking, Barbara Jo came home. "Well, hi Gordie!" She said with a smile, as she tugged off her boots and walked stocking foot to the refrigerator.

Gordie had trouble responding and could hardly breathe from the sight of grown-up Barbara Jo. *She's a knockout,* he thought.

The knockout pulled up a chair to join them around the kitchen table and make a sandwich. Gordie relaxed, smiled, and told stories that made her laugh.

Before long, Bob, the opportunist, chimed in to say, "Hey, Gordie! Whadda you think about hanging around here more often, helping out and doing some chores?

Gordie work at Country Club Ranches had a lot to do with seeing Barbara Joand he became a trusted regular hand on the property, doing hard work with Michael. The boys became good buddies, and Gordie became like a second son. He often ate dinners with Maxine and the kids, sometimes staying throughout the evening and watching television together.

Gordie's yearnings for Barbara Jo were a futile fantasy. He asked her out on dates, but Barbara Jo always said no. Gordie's status as a family friend put the kibosh on Barbara Jo's romantic interest. Gordie could never resolve that dilemma and just hid his crush.

In 1966 Barbara Jo ran for Rodeo Queen of Broward County confident in her skills to take the title. Competitors sashayed their horse in a polite lope in the contest arena one by one. She entered the show ring on a blue-eyed albino white stallion circling the judges in a full gallop. For her finale, the stallion reared up, dropped down, and took a bow. She wore a lovely lavender cowgirl suit and like royalty, won the crown.

Barbara Jo graduated from Miami Carol City High School, Dade County, 1967 and enrolled in Broward Junior College in the pursuit of higher education. She saw a veterinarian degree as the right track for her future. But on one fateful day, another track came along that changed everything.

"I know your secret."

Her dad spoke between a raspy cough and sipping black coffee at the kitchen table, recovering from a bender.

The room held a silent pause before he continued, "I know about your match racing for Warman back when. Did you think I wouldn't find out?"

Barbara Jo stood as her dad's words seemed to cave in around her. She froze into the uncertainty of what was next.

"And, you gave it up?" Bob slapped his own forehead then smiled to say. "You were good enough to win, right?"

She boldly pointed out, "It's illegal! Anyway, I'm doing what I should do now."

Bob's eyes narrowed as he whispered, "Why would you quit something that you're good at?"

"It's just a dream...me becoming a jockey." She waited for a scathing reaction.

Bob merely said, "So, do it."

Bob's ulterior motive for his daughter's jockey dream is speculative but regardless, he was an important steppingstone in his daughter's jockey career.

Bob phoned his nephew, Robert. Robert Burns was a lawyer who owned six racehorses. Burns had street grit in his blood from his prize-fighter dad, Bobby and owed his Uncle Bob a favor. Burns quickly up a meeting for his second cousin, Barbara Jo, to meet his racehorse trainer at Tropical Park.

Inside the racetrack property, Barbara Jo saw the culture all around her; so many beautiful horses, the grandstand, the barns – up close and personal. She thought to herself, *"Wow, I'm really here!* She stepped on sacred ground for the first time.

Burns escorted Barbara Jo and Bob to the track backside, where the heart of the racetrack beats with the activity of grooms, jockeys, exercise riders, hot walkers and trainers. The backside is an assembly line of racehorse care in various stages of stall cleaning, feeding, grooming, cool downs and farrier services. Racehorses outnumbered people in majestic amounts.

Among the hustle and bustle of riders getting on and off horses going back and forth to the track for morning workouts, Barbara Jo watched how after the horses were worked and hosed off, their pulsing sweaty muscles made steam that evaporated off their bodies and glistened in the morning sun.

Robert introduced his horse trainer, Dave Harper, and him to bring out a Thoroughbred to gallop. Harper gave a somber hello and nodded over (what he assumed was) a dog and pony show for the owner. A bay gelding was led from the stall to tack up.

Harper informed Burns, "Dontae Charm will be ready in no time, boss. Eduardo's galloping today and will breeze him out along the rail past you and your family."

Burns replied, "Uh huh, but we don't need Eduardo. Barbara Jo here will do the riding".

Harper's eyes bulged and he questioned, "Huh?"

"Yeah, we're giving her a try", Burns casually mentioned.

Harper's voice grew louder, "What? A gallop girl?"

Tension rose from zero to one hundred degrees between Burns and Harper. Their voices roared in a boisterous argument. The Rubins stepped outside the barn but heard Burns lowering the boom with a stern threat to take all his horses to another trainer. Harper conceded and saved his meal ticket.

"Alright. Get her on a helmet." Harper stated.

Bob grabbed a helmet off the barn rack and pushed in into his daughter's hands. He then stepped into Harper's face to say, "I'm real glad you came around, Mr. Harper".

Harper chided, "She does have a license?"

Bob squinted and said with a sigh, "Just get the horse out to the track."

The exercise license legally permitting Barbara Jo on the racetrack wouldn't be overlooked, but for the moment, Harper did what he was told. And Barbara Jo was led on the horse to the racetrack.

Harper motioned for assistance from a track staff and when close enough for instruction, Harper squealed about the unlicensed girl on the horse.

The man shook his head, huffed and puffed shouting, "Wait a minute! You mean you ain't got an exercise license? Ah, no, no, NO. You got no business being on this track!"

The audition was cut short. Burns didn't want to make a public fuss, so the entourage made a U-turn back to the barn, and there, Burns laid down the law. Harper would file Barbara Jo's paperwork at the track office as a gallop rider. for Burns' horses immediately. Harper would comply to give Barbara Jo a chance, or else.

The matter of Barbara Jo's horse racing ambition relied on following the rules right now, not breaking them. This formality was easy, since ladies did exercise Thoroughbreds, just not run them in a race. The women who galloped racehorses were typically, trainers' wives or daughters.

As Barbara Jo trotted back to the barn, in the saddle of a Thoroughbred she had a seat at the top of her world. The horses' prancing stride felt elegant and strong. The equine athlete glided along the sandy track footing like an ice skater.

Every part of Barbara Jo was electrified from the motion and the grace she was connected to. In sync with the rhythmic breathing and serene confidence of the horse, her body balanced with its shifting muscles, like a second skin.

Harper did not like being out ranked and he especially didn't like the idea of a female gallop rider. His red-hot Irish temper probed Burns, "Don't I have any say so?"

Burns listened to Harper demand for Barbara Jo to muck stalls, clean tack, hot walk and groom all six horses, pro bono. After the barn chores were done first, she would exercise one Thoroughbred. Harper would escort her ride on a pony beside her tethered with a lead rope, *'cuz he didn't want to be the blame for her breaking her neck.*

Barbara Jo spoke up for the first time in the morning's ordeal to reply, "Ok, that's no problem".

Robert Burns gave his cousin a wink.

She whispered back, "Thank you".

Barbara Jo dropped out of her junior college classes to enroll in the racing track school of hard knocks. It was humbling. First, she learned how much she didn't know.

The Thoroughbred measures 15.2 up to 17H (hands) tall. This bold breed is distinguished by its powerful haunches, spacious chest, long forelegs, lean muscles and sleek coat.

Thoroughbred ancestry is traced back to three racing horses imported to England in the 18th century and named for their respective owners; the Byerley Turk, the Darley Arabian and the Godolphin Arabian. The Thoroughbred requires an expert rider who can confidently channel the energy of the world's fastest horse breed.

Working with Harper was no walk in the park. He used lingo without explanation and rarely held a civil conversation. When he spoke, he yelled. Nevertheless, Barbara Jo came in early every morning; always got her work done first, maintained a good attitude and learned by everything going on around her.

Harper was not an example of a great trainer, but Barbara Jo was educated on all the other things she needed to know. She learned the rein configurations of half cross and full cross and became familiar with iron lengths that were adjusted for the counterclockwise circular racetrack, different from match race stirrups on a straight away.

A popular stirrup setup technique made famous by jockey Eddie Arcaro is called acey-deucey. The inside leg iron length is set longer than the outside leg for better balance around the high-speed racetrack turns. It became second nature to set stirrups (irons) and tie up the reins for training workouts.

Galloping was thrilling. Barbara Jo wasn't scared or nervous doing it, just ambitious to master it. The sensation of riding the wind from the back of a horse made her blood tingle. She loved to feel the powerful pace of the racing stride. Her balance was instinctive, but she needed to develop her leg muscles like never before and build up her upper arm muscles further.

It was a glorious feeling to be in sync with the Thoroughbred, and she grew a deep respect for its perfect power. Within three weeks, Barbara Jo galloped without Harper's tether line. Harper made the decision by his own admission; she proved that his apron strings were never really needed.

The backside of a racetrack is a hardworking and macho environment. Exercise women heard dirty and gritty language. These women were reminded how they were considered bad luck for just being on the backside due to superstitious beliefs.

Superstitions are not facts, yet they are endorsed. Horses had the same problem. An old saying considered white legs (socks & hooves) of a horse to be bad luck. California Chrome (with white legs) crushed the 2014 Kentucky Derby proving that talent (Chrome was a descendant of Secretariat) overcomes obstacles. Where high priced well-bred racehorses are concerned, diligent care is a must for the best results. Barbara Jo found a wealth of knowledge and friendship from the black grooms on the track. These men were intelligent, especially sensitive and generous to share their gift of expertise to her.

Thoroughbreds are well made for speed and efficient use of energy, but racing is tough on them. The grooms had taught Barbara Jo how to take special care of legs and hooves.

The *no hoof no horse* adage, was a golden rule. It is imperative to keep the horse sound under the impact and pressure of both training and racing. Going lame (injured) causes medical expenses, time and drains profits for trainers and owners.

The average Thoroughbred has the metabolism of a thirteen-year-old boy, and Barbara Jo learned about proper racehorse nutrition. She became educated in jockey gear, horserace tack, and the rules of racing while working on the backside. She was exactly where she needed to be to get to where she dreamt of going.

She caught on quickly to track politics. A day didn't go by without someone harassing, flirting or making it very clear that she wasn't wanted around. Some rude men cupped their hands on her crouch to "leg up" into the saddle - and that had to be accepted as just another day at work for her. A smart woman had to choose her battles, and she would do hers in a race when the time came.

During her one daily gallop, Barbara Jo met another exercise rider, Ronnie Gaffney. He was a loud and popular fella; rough around the edges but kindhearted. Gaffney was also of good horseracing stock, related to Jimmie Gaffney, who was Secretariats' gallop rider.

They hung out socially and shared mutual horse and racing interests. They weren't dating, but Barbara Jo didn't mind if others thought they were an item because that shut down gratuitous come ons. Their social friendship concluded when Tropical Park's racing season ended.

Harper headed to the New England circuit at Suffolk Downs for more racing with Burn's horses. Barbara Jo figured out a way to head north, too. She asked a lady hot walker, Donna, to share a room on Revere Beach for twenty-five dollars a week within walking distance of the racetrack. The girls split expenses, which was the only way Barbara Jo could afford to go. Harper wasn't excited about her tagging along but was happy about the free labor.

The days were hard, and the work was tough in Boston. Like all the racetracks in this era, they were prone to devastating fires. The buildings, grandstands, barns, and roofs were made of wood and often very close to each other. The backside housed large amounts of hay and straw bedding, giving plenty of flammable material to burn things away quickly.

Arriving at Suffolk Downs on a late fall day for their four am workout, Barbara Jo and Donna smelled dense smoke.

The dawn was breaking the night's darkness with flickers of embers floating in the air like sparklers, but this was no celebration.

Once they got to the backside, they saw firetrucks hosing flames engulfing the horse barns and the flares of emergency vehicles on the scene. Firefighters were saving a barn that was newly built out of cinder blocks.

Barbara Jo was nauseated by the smell of charred horses and saw a horse (named Reely Beeg) run from its burning barn with his back on fire.

It was rumored that the fire was arson deliberately set to threaten a trainer, named Bryan Webb, for his questionable business dealings. Webb stabled nearly thirty horses in the cinder block barn, and some perished. However, Reely Beeg survived and healed from skin grafts to return to racing.

Barbara Jo made no income in Boston and with little savings left to pay rent; she could barely buy food. It was common for her to show up at the track dining room during meals asking patrons, *"are you going to eat that?"* and savor what was given away. She stayed hungry, a lifestyle to get used to for becoming a jockey.

"Anyone here wanna gallop for me?"

On a gloomy rainy morning, Barbara Jo heard a yell over the cracks of thunder. The voice carried through the barn shed rows where exercise riders and trainers waited for the storm to break. The severe rainstorm intensified with lightning but trainer, Bill Siravo wouldn't wait. "ANYONE?" the yell beckoned.

Barbara Jo volunteered, "Yeah, I will".

Siravo walked up to her, emphasizing. "I'm not gonna sugar coat this, this one is a tough gallop, and he doesn't like this weather, but I gotta get him worked now for his race tomorrow. Are you *sure* that you can gallop a tough horse?"

"Yes, I sure can" she answered.

It hailed while Barbara Jo mounted Siravo's big bay horse. They trotted onto the track with both their heads tucked down low. The horse was hesitant to work but trusted his rider. They galloped against the storm that now included hail. Barbara Jo's sight line was so limited that she couldn't see the rail poles to gauge distance and timing. They ran a steady and safe pace on the mushy footing of the water-logged track.

"Just keep going, you're doing fine", Barbara Jo repeated out loud to soothe herself and the horse.

The squall blasted after Barbara Jo galloped, ruining daily workouts for everybody else except Siravo. Bill Siravo complimented Barbara Jo for taking the job that no one else wanted to do and for doing it well.

"I don't think I was all that impressive", she explains in hindsight, "the horse just listened to me."

Her gallop made an impression on Siravo, who immediately offered Barbara Jo a paying job with him. She took the offer and said good-bye to her free labor position with Harper. Bill Siravo was the next step that she needed.

The forty-something-year-old Italian was a good man to work for, had a wonderful smile and a knack for training. He owned the big, beautiful horses that he trained and adored them all. Siravo's main business was operating a produce market in

Rhode Island where he lived, and he frequently invited Barbara Jo to his home to share meals alongside his family.

She loved training at the New England meet. It was fantastic except for the winter weather. Galloping in the severely cold temperatures was especially hard for the Floridian to get used to. Siravo's respectful attitude and understanding of her talent gave her strength to do the unbearable. Others took notice of her emerging brilliance on the track, too.

Trainer Bryan Webb recovered from the Boston barn fire setback. He raced at Rockingham Park in Salem New Hampshire and unloaded a horse named, Be Dashing, in a claiming race to Siravo.

Be Dashing was a hot mess. He was a small, skinny horse with a nervous personality. He paced in his stall to the point of exhaustion. Dashing's troubled nature would not let him relax or keep on a healthy weight.

Siravo had an idea to quiet down Be Dashing. He mounted a mirror inside Be Dashing's stall, and the little guy was comforted by the reflection of another horse for company. Once rested and with weight on, Be Dashing was ready for Barbara Jo to gallop him.

Be Dashing was not only a nervous Nellie, but he galloped unusually by lowering his head only about a foot off the ground. Previous gallop riders took a big hold on the reins to bring his head up, which soured him to force. Be Dashing had a habit of bearing down on the bit and running off. His refusal to be controllable on the track made him poor racing talent.

On their first workout, Barbara Jo casually sang out loud and felt Be Dashing relax. She stopped and started her serenade a few times to test Be Dashing's response. Each time she sang, the horse responded cooperatively.

She brought him into a gallop and allowed him to run in his unusual way and did not interfere or try to pull his head up. When she cued to breeze, (asked to run the fastest) Be Dashing then naturally pulled up his head to balance a stronger stride. He became attentive and confident during workouts and showed enough improvement to be entered in a higher claiming race.

Barbara Jo ponied him to the starting gate, talking gently and calmly to Be Dashing. The jockey noticed their connection.

"What else works on him?" The jockey questioned.

Knowledge is power in any sport. Generous with her skill and expertise, Barbara Jo told the jockey not to pull on his mouth in the race. "Let him find his stride at the gate break and he'll do the work and win".

The jockey followed her secrets and Be Dashing broke on top leading the pack to the finish line, just as predicted. Claimed to new owners, Be Dashing's continued success won his next two races, moving up in class to win an allowance race.

Webb was sure that nobody could remedy any of his "bad" horses' racing performances and made a point to introduce himself to Barbara Jo at Rockingham Park.

Webb walked into Siravo's barn, "Barbara Jo". I'm Bryan Webb." Bryan Webb was a husky and healthy guy, but his eyes revealed a hunger. He made an offer to her to work exercising his thirty horses. The deal came with over twice the current money she made, but Barbara Jo didn't contemplate it.

She shook his hand, saying, "It's nice to meet you, Mr. Webb, but no thanks. I've got a really good thing with Mr. Siravo".

Webb cleared his throat and answered, "Suit yourself". And added, "But I'd have you working back in Florida."

The Florida seasonal meet between Tropical Park, Hialeah and Gulfstream racetracks were good stakes and a great opportunity. Webb's breath left a frosty cloud floating in the air as Barbara Jo tucked her wool cap over her ears, zipped her coat and walked away.

Siravo, Barbara Jo and horses followed races further north to Lincoln Downs, Rhode Island. Barbara Jo enjoyed the benefits of supporting herself as a gallop girl. She didn't splurge on much but occasionally paid for long-distance calls home to check in.

While on the phone with her mom, Bob grabbed the phone and asked, "How's it going for you up east? "Where you staying at? I'll be up there for some business, and I'll visit."

Barbara Jo gave her address - doubting he would show up. Bob arrived at her apartment drunk and disorderly, and she brushed him off while on her way to her early morning workout.

By mid-morning at the track, Barbara Jo spotted a group of fellows in dark overcoats and hats standing along the rail. *That's unusual*, she thought.

Concerned and curious she rode over to the group to ask, "Everything ok?"

One of the men, dressed like a head undertaker, answered casually, "Just checking up on you for your dad".

Bill Siravo was there at the rail too, a comfortable distance away from the group of men. He motioned for Barbara Jo and in a hushed tone grilled her, "What are you doing talking to those men?"

She told him verbatim what was said and then asked, "Why?"

"Barbara Jo, those guys are connected", Bill cautioned.

"Connected to what?"

"The mob" Bill continued, "That guy you were talking to is Gerry Ouimette. Let's move on".

Criminals shadowed Barbara Jo's life on and off the racetrack. Years later, she connected the dots between Bob Rubin's business trip to Rhode Island, Gerry Ouimette at the track rail and of her grandfather's hot Cadillac deal with her dad.

Gerald Ouimette was known as "The Frenchman" in the organized crime circle. Ouimette's entry job for the Patriarca New England crime family was stealing and selling Cadillac's. Stolen cars were Ouimette's early calling card for felonious business.

A winter on the Northeastern circuit was tougher than Barbara Jo could imagine, and it worsened when Siravo trained and raced at Lincoln Downs in Rhode Island. She bundled up as best as possible while remaining agile and light to gallop.

During those dawn morning workouts, the cold iron stirrups cut like razor blades through her leather boots, and the winter rain pierced her like bullets. Her gloves stuck to the leather reins and snot froze on her face under the riding mask. She became homesick for the sunshine and temperature of Florida. Bryan Webb's offer to work in Florida came to mind. She phoned him to discuss further details of the contract.

"Hello. This is Barbara Jo Rubin. Bryan, remember when you offered me a job exercising for you?".

"Oh yeah," Webb answered. "Have you come to your senses to get out of that damn cold and work for me in Florida?"

"Yes, I have...but with one condition." Barbara Jo continued, "I want to be a jockey and ride races."

Webb didn't hesitate to answer, "When are you coming?"

Barbara Jo was at the Tropical Park racing office within days for the official business necessary to work under contract with Webb and to complete the jockey apprentice license as track rules required. The racing office administrator reviewed her documents and noticed the apprentice license.

"Looks like you made a mistake. *You* can't get an apprentice jockey license."

"But I need it. Why not?" She questioned.

He maintained, "Because you're a woman, that's why."

She left the office with just the exercise rider's license realizing that her dream was bigger than just ability. For the moment, it was blocked by a barrier that neither Webb nor she had power over. Regardless, Barbara Jo banked on the benefits of training a bigger variety of horses for their personal best; it perfected her capabilities, and she sharpened her focus on the starting gate.

On the back of a racehorse standing inside the two-foot wide by six-foot-long starting stall, is much like sitting on a keg of dynamite inside a closet. Serious injuries and fatalities can occur at the starting gate moments before the race starts, and horse panic can spread like wildfire causing injuries like dominos.

Inside the starting gate Barbara Jo keenly noticed how the horses subtly twitched their ears at the imperceptible sound (to humans) of the electromagnetic gate spring clicking a split second before the starting bell rang as the gates opened.

Barbara Jo Rubin on Stoneland, Bryan Webb 1969

Barbara Jo watched for the ear twitch, held her position and burst out becoming a master of a clean break. Moments count in every race and much like life; timing is everything.

Chapter 3

Breaking the Glass Gate

It's hard to fit in when you are meant to stand out.
– Dr Seuss

Olympian equestrian, Kathy Kusner, decided to also participate in the sport of horse racing as a jockey in 1967, She applied to the Maryland Racing Commission for her license. She was turned down.

On her way to court, armed with the 1964 Civil Rights Act, Kusner declared, "Horse riding is more of technique and skill than strength. It's the same as playing chess with men, so I don't intend to give up the fight".

The 1964 Civil Rights Act, signed by President Lyndon Johnson forbids discrimination in employment because of sex, race, national origin, or religion. Kusner's year-long legal battle concluded when Judge Ernest A. Loveless, overturned the Racing Commission's ruling. "This court finds that no reasonable mind could possibly have reached the factual conclusion that the Maryland Commission did." Loveless ordered a reversal of the ruling on the grounds that Kusner's license had been refused on the basis of sex discrimination.

Earlier in 1968, the Kentucky Racing Commission granted a license to Penny Ann Early. Yet, neither woman made it to the gates to become the first female jockey. Early was boycotted at Churchill Downs, and Kusner broke her leg.

Female jockeys were vying for racing on horse tracks but that felt like treading water on a sinking ship. Tropical Park didn't see it coming when Barbara Jo applied for her apprentice's jockey license, but the wheels were in motion, and the times were changing.

American Civil Liberties Union activist, Dru Doescher Sellars, heard how Barbara Jo Rubin's apprentice jockey application was denied, and she took on the rejection with a legal case.

Sellars, along with Robert Burns won a court order ruling that forced Tropical Park to process Barbara Jo's apprentice jockey license application and have the license expedited to the Florida Racing Commission for review.

It was standard procedure and the responsibility of the Florida Racing Commission to mitigate danger and verify a rider's ability during a trial race. But in an unprecedented step, the commission also called for a private meeting with the foreboding female apprentice jockey before a trial race to investigate whether Barbara Jo held a personal agenda to promote the Equal Rights Amendment for women which was spearheading the country's political arena.

The committee's interview was brief, and Barbara Jo assured them of her authentic professional ambition to become a jockey. She asserted that her talent at the trial race would show proof.

For the trial race, the commission officials lined up in the grandstand. Webb rode his pony horse alongside Barbara Jo and her mount. They nodded to the officials and jogged to the starting gate.

The gate crew loaded her into the starting gate along with two journey jockeys as challengers. Barbara Jo broke clean from the start and held the lead down the backside.

Around the first turn Barbara Jo's horse switched lead perfectly as she drove to the rail position. On the second turn for the stretch, she pushed the lead and rode to the wire successfully.

The stewards unanimously endorsed her capability, and the Florida Racing Commission issued her apprentice jockey license immediately. Barbara Jo was deemed ready for an official horse racing entry. All indications pointed toward the eminent debut appearance of a female jockey entering the sport of horse racing very soon.

During this time, Barbara Jo detected a familiarity with Bryan Webb. Her trainer reminded her of her dad; both were alcoholics and gamblers and often involved in shady dealings. Bob Rubin and Bryan Webb knew each other and didn't mix well. They even looked alike. Both men resembled the American actor, Robert Mitchum.

While working for Webb at Tropical Park, she resided with her parents at Country Club Ranches. Barbara Jo's dad dropped her off to the track daily, and she just assumed that he left the track and went elsewhere with his day.

However, she found out that Bob hustled pool at Tropical Park first, before leaving. He was a shark with his one-handed and left-handed tricks, which was no surprise to Barbara Jo, but his pool schemes caused repercussions.

Bob swindled money from guys that Barbara Jo worked around, and he boasted about his daughter (the jockey), while doing so. It's hard to make friends at work when your dad is hustling money from them. Barbara Jo merely noted to herself that her dad was really good at being bad. She had seen a fair share of sketchy masculine characters and was incredulous around most men.

That fact didn't help matters for her friend Gordie, who still pined for her. While working for Bob at Country Club Ranches, Gordie witnesses Barbara Jo's intensity and balance with horses. And often wondered why horses were the only thing she allowed to get close to her.

Horses appeal to a variety of people, ranging from farm folks to royalty. The sport of horse racing is a fast and glorious exhibition of combined equine and human talent. Rules are easy to understand, and gamblers place bets by reasoning, a hunch or a tip and win or lose in a moment's notice.

But what was now newsworthy about horse racing was how it entered a social and political frontline with women in the sport. On January 15, 1969, Bryan Webb entered his horse, Stoneland, on Tropical Park's afternoon program with Barbara Jo Rubin as the jockey.

Previous women who had applied to work as jockeys during 1968-1969, forged a path for others and Barbara Jo was taking her turn.

Barbara Jo was judged like a filly's conformation at an auction, and the nineteen-year-old was naive, but ready. Early articles described the rookie and her clothes as sexy, and mentioning her credentials paragraphs later. During this time Webb duly pointed out that all she needed was a chance to race. In truth, what she needed more was protection.

Horses understand protection. A solitary herd animal is often considered easy prey. If alone, a horse can and will defend itself but fairs much better in the safety of a herd.

Barbara Jo's signature brunette pig tail braids and Mary Tyler Moore sophisticated beauty, dazzled. Her athletic 5"6' frame towered over the average 4"10' jockey height. It was her talent and passion to ride in the male dominated king of sports that she stood out as both a hero and a villain. Everyone watched and waited for the story to unfold.

With her first official race entry scheduled, her world hadn't changed much, yet. Barbara Jo promptly started her day for

Webb and the long routine of training. Bryan ran the show of instructing exercise riders, grooms and barn help. Barbara Jo always looked forward to getting in the saddle for her first gallop workouts. But now, while minding to her job she was interrupted, "Barbara Jo, look this way!"

Newsmen lined up at the track rail snapping pictures and requesting interviews. She ignored the hubbub and focused on her work. Webb didn't seriously respond to a rumor of a race boycott at Tropical Park. He only advised Barbara Jo that if the fraternity refused to ride, she would (by racing rules), take the win in a walk-over race.

A walk-over race rules victory to the jockey who commits to racing after scratch time, even if they were the only rider. But the disgrace of victory given to a girl jockey, without a field of competitors would be counterproductive to the human male ego.

Races at Tropical Park during the Florida winter meet were spectacular and similar to the splendor of a May derby day. The sunny and mild south Miami weather always hosted a program full of talent, gambling, and good sport.

On January 15, the unprecedented gate attendance of 11,000 spectators came to see what had never been seen; a female jockey ride. Crowds that large are a peculiar thing. It floods the premises with a tidal wave of energy and as the tide moves in closer to take a picture, ask a question or yell a comment, it seems to suck out the air.

Going to work as an apprentice jockey kept unfolding. On this milestone race, she had a police escort to get her through the boisterous crowd, a crowd that yelled out both comments of encouragement and condemnation.

"Good luck."

"Get yourself a husband!"

"Go home and make babies".

"You belong in the kitchen."

"Right on lady!"

"Go get them yellow bellies!"

She mentally squeezed out distractions and walked through the crowd to a trailer parked outside in the jocks' yard. This wasn't a Hollywood star luxury trailer; it was a necessity. There were no female dressing rooms on racetracks yet.

As the outside ruckus clamored, Barbara Jo dressed in her racing silks and met with the track doctor, who appeared quite nervous, placing his stethoscope near her bosom to listen to her heart. She weighed in at the scales and waited. There was a moment she thought; *this is finally going to happen,* and in the familiar territory of the thundering hooves she counted down to herself, *ready or not, here I come.*

Tropical Park boycott race 1969

The Tropical Park owner, Saul Silberman, got very nervous. at what was appearing to happen. He pulled Bryan Webb aside admitting that he didn't want the girl to ride and stir up things.

Webb trained horses for Silberman, and he conceded since a race boycott meant no betting, and no betting meant no revenue. and that the crowds' anger could be disastrous for Tropical Park. The "solution" was officially announced over the track public address system,

Due to the refusal of the male riders to ride against a girl because of the danger they believed to be involved, Bryan Webb, of his own volition, has substituted a male jockey, Jorge Velasquez, in order to keep racing going at Tropical Park.

The crowd both booed and cheered at the news. The threat of a riot in the grandstand was not an exaggeration, but neither was the determination of this female jockey to run a race.

Barbara Jo's attorney (cousin) Robert Burns gave his legal insight over the situation on the spot, declaring, "The action of the jockeys is a conspiracy and is abominable. But they're fighting a losing cause against the law of the land. If Barbara is not given a chance to ride within a reasonable time, I will file an anti-trust suit against the Jockey's Guild and individual suits against the riders in circuit court."

Tropical Park's General Manager, Elmer Vickers, shared to the press his opinion of the boycott, "My faith in humanity has been shaken"

Track Steward, Ed Pons commented, "We (the stewards) are not at all satisfied with this action by the jockeys. It appears to be a violation of the rules of racing. When the riders failed to take themselves off their mounts by scratch time this morning, they in effect, made a commitment to ride. They failed to faithfully fulfill their engagement."

George D. Johnson Jr. the Florida Supervisor of Racing counter cited, "They did fulfill their engagements when a girl was replaced with a male". The media pounced on the story of anti-trust litigations, state racing rule violations, civil liberties, and equal rights.

Reporters covered the legal facts and opinions about the gender divide. Jockeys and trainers shared comments.

"If she has the guts to do it, I say, let her ride. I'd ride against her."

"They break horses from the gates in the mornings against male jockeys and you don't hear the boys objecting. Why should the boys say no when they put the money on the line in the afternoon?"

"If women want to ride, let them. Time will tell if they are qualified to compete against men. Let them prove it".

"Some girls can ride okay, especially if they get horses that only need a light touch. But the ones that take heavy handling give a girl trouble."

"Would I ride against a girl...why not? And if she tried to come through inside on the rail, I'd nail her if I could. If a girl wants to come into a man's game, she's got to play by the man's rules."

Jockey's Guild Representative, Ward Sigler, gave his thoughts, "I felt it was discriminating. I felt that she should have the opportunity".

Future inductee of The National Museum of Racing Hall of Fame, Angel Cordero Jr., made his comment stating, "I would race against her. Everybody else thinks of her as a girl. I think of her as a jockey".

Cordero came from a family of horse racing professionals in Puerto Rico. He saw prejudice and had to work hard when he hit the states in 1962, before making his mark in horse racing history. The most requested comment about the boycott race was Barbara Jo's. "I'm very disappointed. I'm not sure what happened, but I'll keep trying to ride. I feel as qualified as any apprentice. If I were a boy, I'd probably fight this thing, too. It's been a man's sport for so long – well, it's traditional. I guess I don't blame them for fighting."

The press reported that the boycotting jockeys acted like a mob. Barbara Jo didn't snitch how the jockeys verbally threatened to "put her over the rail" and about the brick thrown through her trailer window while she waited inside.

At the end of the boycott race, Barbara Jo left the track with her chin up and rode home with her beau, Billie McKeever.

Billie, an eighteen-year-old second-generation Arkansas jockey was caught up in the dilemma. He appeared sensitive to Barbara Jo's disappointment and gave Barbara Jo a cavalier shrug musing "Well, whatever happens, happens".

Looking at them together, you might see a budding romance. Barbara Jo and Billie met at Pimlico racetrack during early morning training. Billie would smile and nod at Barbara Jo, while jogging horses back and forth from the track to the backside. When Billie took the initiative to ask the lady apprentice out for a date and she accepted. Before long, they were courting exclusively.

Barbara Jo liked dating Billie and especially liked the fact that he wasn't a drinker. Billie's dark hair and slender 5"8' chassis was handsome, but he lacked the maturity and sensibility that Barbara Jo easily sported.

They were both young and talented. She was at the brink of becoming a pioneer female jockey and Billie was the 1968 Arkansas Derby stakes winner. Life's timing would break up their courtship's survival.

While it lasted, they were good natured to each other along their star-crossed romance in the world of horse racing careers. Billie's fate would become sorted; ending with a questionable accidental drowning death in 1982 that urban myth linked to the Boston mob.

Immediate action was taken by the Florida Racing Commission against the Tropical Park boycott incident. Thirteen jockeys were fined one hundred dollars each for refusing to ride their race entry after scratch time.

The event caught the attention of George Capron, a horse owner in the Bahamas. Capron commissioned Arthur Foulkes, the Bahamas Minister of Tourism to invite Barbara Jo to enter riding at Nassau's Hobby Horse Hall racetrack.

She accepted the race entry on January 25, 1969. The race brought friends, family, and fans to Nassau. However, her work visa was delayed and she was scratched – but she didn't waste the trip.

Barbara Jo got acquainted with the Nassau racing culture, met Nassau track officials, and studied track films. She realized how narrow the jocks rode the lanes and how tightly they squeezed each other, rallying for the rail position. She also noted that the island jockeys had no complaints about racing against her.

Nassau Bahamas, 1969

The Hobby Horse Hall official race took place on January 28. Her work visa was authorized, and exuberant fans anticipated a lady jockey racing debut. Hobby Horse Hall heavily promoted the race event and with no politics in the way; the press merely noted her professional composure before the race, compared racing conditions and waited for results.

Barbara Jo rode the gallant island mare, Flyaway. At the starting gate, she pulled down her racing goggles and talked softly to Flyaway while the field loaded. She grabbed a handful of mane, watched the ear twitch and looked out into the backstretch ahead. The moment was serene.

"AND THEY'RE OFF!

Flyaway broke clean from the gate, taking the lead. Internal tranquility lasted throughout the race, and all Barbara Jo heard was Flyway's steady breathing and thunder-pulsing hooves. Around the second turn to the finish line, Flyaway listened to her rider's cue to stay at the lead. Barbara Jo glanced back at the field and knew if Flyaway kept the pace they would be first to the wire, by three lengths.

History was made.

Barbara Jo heard the roar of the fans at the finish line yelling *for* her, not at her. She raised up in the stirrups and held her whip up in the air for a timeless jockey moment. This was the first female jockey to win a Thoroughbred pari-mutuel race sanctioned by the American Racing Association.

Pulling up, she patted Flyaway lovingly on the neck saying, "Good girl. What a good girl! I knew you would win!"

Flyaway loped to the winner's circle where Webb congratulated Barbara Jo with a kiss on her cheek. The track race board lit up officially declaring her first place. The crowds' revelry exploded in pandemonium, and people charged her tearing parts of her silks for a memento.

Security cleared a path to get her off the track, but first Barbara Jo threw her racing goggles out to the crowd. The fan hysteria didn't compare to her inner joy from riding and winning her first race at last.

"I was more overcome with relief than excitement. What I believed and worked for was proven; that I was good enough to win a horse race." Barbara Jo notes with heartfelt reflection, "I was a jockey."

The victor stabled at Pimlico Racetrack in Baltimore, Maryland with sights for race entries at the east coast meet. She resided at the Reisterstown Hotel in an efficient room near the track. Training in the morning dawn, news crews, spectators and horsemen watched her from the Pimlico grandstand.

Webb obtained an overnight entry for Barbara Jo at Laurel Park Race Track, Maryland, and he requested a work dinner together for a discussion. She arrived at the diner where Webb was seated and waiting and plopped down in the booth and quickly asked concerned, "Okay, just tell me, what's going on. Are they going to boycott again?"

Webb slurred when he said, "No, no, there's nothing wrong, darling".

She was familiar with the forty two-year old trainer being drunk, so she kept the conversation focused on the race. While waiting respectfully for answers, Webb filled his coffee cup with oaky bourbon from his worn and tattered silver flask.

Webb complimented her talent and emphasized his role in her success. His words dripped with sarcasm and left a sadistic implication that - *you owe me.*

Barbara Jo got uncomfortable and made her exit.

"Well, I'm really tired. The morning is gonna be a very early start. I need to get as much sleep as I can.... I'm going back to my room now. See you in the morning at the barn."

Webb said, "Oh? Yeah, you're right. I better get going, too. C'mon, let's walk you back to your room".

He was quiet as they walked across the street to the hotel.

"Goodnight, Mr. Webb. See ya in the morning," Barbara Jo turned her back while unlocking her room.

A dense thump slammed her head into the door, causing a second of darkness. Webb collided into her like an NFL linebacker and pinned her against the door groping at her from behind.

STOP it! What are you doing!!" She screamed.

He puffed like an old bull pawing at the nineteen-year-old and was grossly aroused. She broke free from his mauling, unlocked the door and bolted it shut.

She held her breath listening as he staggered away, then dry heaved. She splashed water on her face at the bathroom sink. The flickering fluorescent light reflected a ghostly image in the mirror as she packed her things and left.

Billie McKeever was happy for her unexpected visit to Arkansas. Barbara Jo didn't tell him what she was running from, only saying that she had to get away.

She watched McKeever win a race and then went back to his place to relax for the rest of the day. McKeever rented a house with other jockeys who were shocked to meet her and didn't even pretend to be courteous. While she was using the restroom, she heard a whisper among the guys.

"This is great Billie....when you marry her and get her knocked up, we won't have to worry about riding against her", they quipped.

Barbara Jo used Billie's house telephone before leaving the scene.

"Hello Mr. Webb, this is Barbara Jo".

It was hard to speak to him. Webb berated her for skipping out on the Laurel Park race to see her boyfriend. She defended herself against his shallow allegation and explained that it was *his* behavior for her reason to leave. Webb denied her story, insisting - that didn't happen. She felt a reminiscent chill.

Her dad would say *this didn't happen,* as a futile attempt to alter the reality of his bad doing with denial. The similarity of Webb and her dad was haunting.

In the meantime, February 7, 1969, at Hialeah Park, Florida, Diane Crump became the first female jockey to ride a race in the United States. It was highly publicized and a great achievement. Diane came in tenth of a twelve-horse field.

Webb taunted Barbara Jo about Crump's notoriety.

"It doesn't matter who was the first to do this. I'm proud that Diane was able to ride," she declared.

Fans saw another woman jockey ride a race. But they didn't see her win.

The winner was on her way

Chapter 4

Riding the Dream

*Your dream has come early but remember
it will have to last you all the rest of your life.*
– National Velvet movie, 1945

Rubin trained and stabled at Pimlico racetrack, although Pimlico resisted a female jockey the entry to ride a race. A one-hour drive west, featured Charles Town Racetrack in West Virginia, where Bryan Webb convincingly booked an evening race entry.

"You know, I've got a girl jockey who could ride here and put Charles Town on the map. This is a nice Jewish girl who can ride. I thought you people took care of your own."

Irvin Kovens, owner of Charles Town Racetrack, thought carefully before he gave permission for Barbara Jo Rubin to race on February 22, 1969. This entry was posted in the ninth race on a six-year-old gelding named Cohesion, whose name

is defined as joining, sticking together - often in reference to healing a wound.

Together, Cohesion and Barbara Jo Rubin did just that.

A jockey agent, Jimmy Fagan, was hired by Webb. The key role of the agent is to find the best horses for the jockey, promote the jockey's ability to the trainer/owner for races. The agent might also make travel arrangements, taxi the jockey, manage media relations, and create buzz for their clients. In Fagan's case, he walked into a pre-made boom.

Prior to race day, team Rubin drove to Charles Town racetrack in West Virginia for her track license. The road trip featured spectacular landscapes of snow-covered ground and frozen waterfalls along the mountains. These were images that Barbara Jo had only seen in travel books.

Barbara Jo was impressed by how Charles Town nestled in the mountains of West Virginia and found the track's six furlongs very lovely.

She introduced herself to fellow jocks on site Those who would talk to her emphasized how sharp the turns are at Charles Town also adding that even journeymen jocks found navigating the track even challenging.

The boys made a big deal of the blustering cold night races, that froze their hands, making it harder to handle the horses. These dilemmas didn't upset Barbara Jo. She figured, if *they can do it, so can I.*

Hordes of journalists kept watch on location at Charles Town the moment the race date was announced, again requiring police escorts for Barbara Jo on the track grounds. The press watched her workouts, took pictures, and requested comments.

Barbara Jo gave interviews and was professionally friendly although brief and concise, telling reporters, "I have to think riding at Charles Town will be a lot safer than it was at Hobby Horse Hall, where the track was really narrow, and the boys didn't look where they were going. I'm sure we'll draw a crowd, and some won't be afraid to bet on me".

Charles Town race night drew a crowd of 9,300, double the usual gate making a record-breaking turnout. The majority seemed to rally for Barbara Jo, although naysayers were vocally in attendance, too.

Track steward Stanley Greene kept the event positive, deflating any gossip of a boycott by emphasizing, "There's no problem from us. She has proven her competence in Florida."

On the night of her race, she used the basement saddle room to dress then napped. The track nurse woke her to weigh in. Harry Roble, her jock valet, laughed when he told reporters, "She's probably the only lady here who had to show her true weight."

Without the distraction of a boycott looming, wagers made Cohesion the favorite to win, with a jockey in top condition. Barbara Jo had studied the opponents' racing form and computed a strategy like an Intel Core i5 processor for her winning outcome. Whether or not that would happen was the very nature of horse racing.

The evening's light rain mixed with the warm enthusiasm of the bursting grandstand. Charles Town was deemed a bull ring track due to the three-quarter mile oval of four very tight turns.

There's a mere 660 feet off the final turn down the last stretch to the finish line.

The race was six & ½ furlongs, so the field break was ½ furlong before the wire passing the grandstand twice. The dirt track condition was wet but solid, keeping it fast. The 34-degree temperature would make the event chilly. Barbara Jo cut off a piece of nylon pantyhose to wear under her helmet to keep her warmer.

She gently spoke to Cohesion as they waited at the starting gate for the rest of the horses to load in. "Now, we got a race to win tonight. So, you do your best and I'll do mine."

In a moment of stillness, the crowd simmered to a murmur. The starting bell rang, and the gates flung open.

Cohesion broke first and led by three lengths. The seven-horse field barreled down the chute. Barbara Jo fell back after the far turn, putting them behind other horses to have a wind shield and conserve Cohesion's loaded energy.

Rival horse, Kathy Keilly, took the lead and Reely Beeg, ran second as Cohesion held fourth position. At the third turn, Kathy Keilly ran wide, giving Reely Beeg the lead. Then Barbara Jo let Cohesion unpack his power to push past Reely Beeg down the home stretch and finished first.

She won the race!

Cohesion paced into the winner's circle with fans cheering. The night twinkled with camera flash bulbs documenting the phenomenon.

Charles Town Race finish line track photo 1969

Barbara Jo commented genuinely with a beautiful smile, "Cohesion did just what I wanted! Mr. Webb told me to get in front and not to worry about the other horses."

Fellow jockey, Diane Crump publicly commented on Barbara Jo's win with excitement, "It makes me feel a mile high".

Charles Town racing steward, Stanley Greene proclaimed, "We'd give her an A on her first performance."

Barbara Jo Rubin and Cohesion, 1969

Barbara Jo made it look easy, but the Charles Town race was not without controversy. The headline read; Apparently Chivalry is Not Dead at Charles Town, insinuating that jockey Larry Kunitake, riding Reely Beeg, gave Cohesion the win.

There were also suspicions about Reely Beeg and Cohesion combined as a single entry (both Webb's horses). The controversial headline caused rumors of an investigation. Webb pushed back against allegations declaring, "Cohesion was a good twenty-five-thousand-dollar horse. He had speed and there was nothing funny about the race."

Barbara Jo quickly pointed out, "Investigation? I've been around too much of that already. Maybe now that I've won all this stuff will stop and people will look at me as a real jockey".

More real female jockeys sprang up to race now that the gender barrier had been cracked open. On March 1, 1969, Diane Crump and Tuesdee Testa both won first place in separate races on the same day. Cheryl White became the first African American jockey, seasoned for her profession by her father, a horse racing trainer.

Robyn Smith rode races successfully before becoming chairman of the NYRA (New York Racing Association). Donna Hillman dropped her modeling career with Harper's Bazaar to race and starred in a Clairol shampoo commercial as a jockey.

Mary Bacon, an Oklahoma tomboy joined jockey ranks and checkered her racing career as a Playboy centerfold and Revlon's Charlie Girl for perfume print ads. Patti Barton, continued beyond this generation of female jockeys with a successful career and passed the torch to her daughter, Donna Barton, who prospered in the vocation.

The new breed of woman jockeys began a lineage, and the lineage would need to age, like a fine wine. Barbara Jo Rubin came out at the start as champagne, but even with the immediate caliber of her professional achievement, it took four years for Rubin to be inducted into the Charles Town Hall of Fame.

Other woman jockeys exist in the shadows of the past because they were never recorded in the Daily Racing form and acknowledged for their merit. Such women came to life in a 2020 special exhibit at the Churchill Downs Museum and live forever in the age of the internet.

The right to ride did not give female jockeys immunity from unscrupulous business deals or tragedy, and in that regard their careers were just like the male jockeys.

Once the phase of boy versus girl, male chauvinism and equal rights cooled off; the horse racing industry was, perhaps, the first to implement gender equality and the controversy increased gate attendance, which didn't go unnoticed.

General Manager of Charles Town Race Track, Charles Funk, spoke about Barbara Jo Rubin telling The Miami Herald, "She rides a nice race. We had a record attendance, and it was because of her."

Barbara Jo Rubin became an overnight sensation. Public interest heralded for appearances, interviews, television shows, and endorsements. The line began to quickly blur between the athlete and the media darling - starting first within her own circle.

Fagan often booked her race entries with tracks that paid appearance fees, a form of kindling to her dream. It would be a matter of time before somebody got burned.

Gordie Gubin was the first to be scorched. As the world was beginning to know Barbara Jo Rubin, Gordie was trying to forget her. Gordie couldn't see himself along for the ride of her ambitious career.

He forced himself to move on and forget about his first crush. Someday he would cast his net for other fish in the sea of love but for now, Gordie enlisted in the Navy and moved on with his young adult life.

Bachelor stallions are a noble type. They are the youthful males of the equine society living on the cusp of their future. When nature fully matures the colts, the stallion forces them out of the herd; the virility of a coming-of-age stallion poses threat to the leader.

In the wild, young studs band together until they find mares. The bachelor herds are comrades of the same club, rivals for the same prize, but safer together along the way. The bachelor stallions learn to fight for the right to compete. Stallions exude magnificent qualities of power and pride. Studies of stallion attributes reveal that they possess a deep sensitivity; especially fond of rewards and appreciation.

Barbara Jo worked for her journeyman's jockey title now. An apprentice jockeys' countdown to the journeyman classification begins with the first career win. After the one-year anniversary of the fifth winning race, an apprentice could then apply for the journeyman's license. Barbara Jo was on her way to her esteemed goal, most likely by 1970.

Simultaneously another position vied for her attention, led by Billie McKeever. He sought media attention for his girlfriend to take a "Mrs." title.

McKeever downplayed her success in the press stating *his* goal for *her*, "I told her to put the reins on me. And to give up riding, this nonsense has got to stop".

His public statement that referred to her career as nonsense and proposing to her publicly didn't go over well with Miss Rubin, who ended the affair after seeing his true colors. Yet, news people pushed further for the scoop questioning her directly, "Miss Rubin, do you have plans of getting married?"

"Of course, but there's plenty of time for that. I'd like to get married and have a nice family, but when that happens, I'll quit racing. It wouldn't be fair to my husband or children."

Questions persisted, "Do you feel your job endangers your femininity?"

"When you're out there you ride to win. You're a jockey. Afterwards, I'm a lady."

Others agreed.

"I'm glad Barbara Jo was the first girl to become successful. Her temperament is right. She's a lady and none of this is going to her head", Barclay Odell, Pimlico's General Manager, told the press and offered her entries for their opening day (finally on board with the concept of female jockeys).

Barbara Jo rode Miss Dee, to win and then placed (second) on Shy Fox, in a photo finish of 60:1 odds. Her parents came from Florida as her guests of honor. They celebrated together despite her dad's drunken behavior in public.

Maxine Rubin and Barbara Jo Rubin 1969

More race entries came quickly. On March 8, 1969, Barbara Jo ran two wins at Waterford Park, West Virginia. She also ran two winners on a single program, twice more at Waterford Park within the same month. The statistics of her apprentice racing performances were spectacular. The grass-roots Rubin team hustled. Barbara Jo is now a very hot commodity.

Webb's newly acquired prestige gave him the gumption to reach out and rub elbows with Howard "Buddy" Jacobson. Buddy Jacobson was the Frank Sinatra of racehorse trainers in New York in the late 1960's.

Horses that Jacobson trained won more races than any other trainer for three consecutive years, and Jacobson stayed in top trainer status for another five years. Horse racing was pure business for Jacobson. Webb's shady business reputation had earned him a lifetime suspension in New York, and he could not race in the empire state. Webb leveraged Barbara Jo's success to open the doors previously barred shut to him.

Frank X. Pagano, Sr., Buddy's right-hand man, answered and screened Webb's phone call to Jacobson. Pagano questioned his boss, "Hey Bud, do you want to talk to Bryan Webb?"

Buddy paused to recognize the name and then accepted. Webb did all the talking and requested Buddy's clout to enter Barbara Jo to ride a race in New York. Jacobson left his decision in the air before committing.

Webb's plan combined bribes and politics, but also Barbara Jo's pure talent. Entering the first woman to ride a horse race at Aqueduct would be historic.

Known as The Big A, Aqueduct was a prominent big purse highly talented track of world class attention. The 210-acre facility resided in the borough of Queens and was named after the grounds of the old Brooklyn Water Works Company.

Buddy discussed Webb's idea with Pagano, starting with some background. "This guy Webb, I've known him for a long time, pretty good trainer…a gambler. He wrote some bad checks or something and can't bring any horses in. He's got an idea. He's got a new broad, some young kid. Wants her to come to New York and ride."

Pagano countered back, "What, are you crazy? A broad in New York? Why should you ride her?"

"Well, times are changing, Frank. You just don't understand. You know half the population is made up of women. Every guy that owns a horse at the track has got a girlfriend or wife or both. I'm telling you Frank; women have got to come to New York. Why shouldn't I be the first guy to give a broad a shot?"

Frank replied, "I think you are nuts, Buddy. All you do is create more controversy."

Jacobson and Pagano met Webb and Barbara Jo at a Maryland restaurant to finalize details, starting with Webb slipped Buddy an envelope of two thousand dollars, which Jacobson referred to as chicken scratch. Buddy and Frank politely stood up and introduced themselves to the young lady. Barbara Jo hardly noticed Buddy's disheveled hair and mucky work shirt; she was more surprised with Webb's crisp shirt and tie.

The dinner conversation established Barbara Jo's debut at Aqueduct, in New York, March 14 and March 15, with Jacobson as the trainer, and Barbara Jo as the jockey. It was a double blessing to compete at Aqueduct and work with the notorious New York trainer.

The association with Buddy Jacobson was controversial throughout his lifetime. Amidst his positive attributes as an esteemed trainer, female jockey proponent and a HBPA (Horsemen's Benevolent and Protective Association) advocate for the benefit and welfare of racetrack backstretch workers, Jacobson's name was also connected to a penchant for young women, drugs, and murder. Buddy died in 1989, at the age of fifty-eight, while serving time for murder at Attica New York State prison.

While working together, Barbara Jo asserts that Buddy was a gentleman to her. Buddy admired Barbara Jo's talent and character during her recent notoriety as the most talked about girl in sports.

She confided, "I'll be happier when all this fuss about a girl jockey is over. I don't feel any different than I did before except I know I'm going to make a lot of mistakes."

There were no mistakes at Aqueduct. Buddy took diligent care of Webb's horse, the maiden filly, Bravy Galaxy. On race day,

Buddy saddled and walked Bravy around the paddock while the large cheering crowd waited for the lady jockey.

She entered the riders up call, and Buddy extended his hand for Barbara Jo's leg up into the saddle. He looked up at her, "Barbara, just go out and do what you can and just be careful."

Barbara Jo Rubin and trainer Buddy Jacobson 1969

Out of the gate like a bullet, number four, Bravy Galaxy took a length lead on the inside. Around the far turn, Barbara Jo kept

Bravy ahead by two lengths. She rode Bravy tight on the rail never drifting and won by two lengths with 13:1 odds.

Bravy Galaxy and Barbara Jo Rubin, Aqueduct 1969

The fans cheered and threw programs in the air. Barbara Jo dismounted and gave Buddy a big hug and kiss on the cheek. The media requested to interview Buddy, but he shook them off and let Barbara Jo be the center of attention.

The next night, Barbara Jo rode Jacobson's horse, May Berry, a seven-year-old chestnut mare. They won the race by three lengths which made all her races at Aqueduct first place wins.

The New York Times ran a picture of Buddy kissing Barbara Jo on the cheek at the winner's circle. Jacobson was so impressed with Barbara Jo that he made an offer to buy out her contract from Bryan Webb. Webb didn't allow it. Buddy's contract offer made her feel valued. However, it was the jockeys at Aqueduct who made her feel accepted.

Angel Cordero Jr. and Barbara Jo Rubin 1969

She raved about them, "This is the best bunch of guys around. They were really great. Angel Cordero, Jr. helped me with my arm number and a couple of guys yelled good luck to me at the gate".

Cordero, Jr. held the honors of initiating her with a bucket of water baptism as a first-time winner. It was the Big A's tradition and an honor. She was dripping wet as Angel leaned in and whispered, "BJ, you gotta lotta heart!" Then he handed her a towel.

The front page of the New York Daily News ran her picture from the Aqueduct race with the headline, That's Why the Lady is a Champ.

Pimlico's racing secretary, Larry Abbundi commented, "Boy (look) what she's done for racing! The last time Aqueduct was on the front page was when that guy was shot in the parking lot." Meaningful moments like riding against Ron Turcotte (Secretariat's jockey), a lifelong friendship with Angel Cordero Jr. and a mink stole that Cohesion's owner, Mr. Lawson, personally gifted to her were not taken for granted. But above all, her talent and determination gave the nineteen-year-old dreamer an incomprehensible satisfaction.

B.J. was her own bookkeeper and recorded her regular weekly exercise pay of $125 per week plus appearance compensation in a leather-bound accountant's ledger that had a faded four-leaf clover taped to the inside cover. Yet, her bank account hardly reflected a fair market value for the accomplishments, and in the end, her lasting equity would only be her name.

Ed Sullivan Show March 1969

Barbara Jo appeared on major prime-time network television programs; The Ed Sullivan Show, Mike Douglas Show, Merv Griffin Show, To Tell the Truth, and Kraft Music Hall.

Global publications; Time, Newsweek, Esquire Magazine, Vogue, LIFE, Cosmopolitan, Coronet and Parade Magazine ran Barbara Jo Rubin stories, pictures and interviews. Daily newspapers kept tabs about her in their sports sections, and horse racing programs and journals reported her races and statistics.

Anchors Walter Cronkite, Hugh Downs, Larry King and Joe Garagiola produced network broadcast features. Garagiola, famously asked the off-color question, "Do girl jockeys wear jock straps?"

She gave a light mannered response, "No. We only wear what's necessary".

Barbara Jo presented the Fiat 124 Sports Spider at the 1969 Madison Square Garden car expo. She made a celebrity endorsement commercial for Metrecal instant food drink.

The luxury watch company, Benrus awarded her the distinguished Benrus Citation Award. She also earned Benrus' Best Time of the Year honor judged by the World Almanac editorial board listing her in the World Almanac

Barbara Jo honored requests for civic appearances at parades, racetracks opening day ceremonies, key-to-the-city presentations, and numerous charity benefits. She fondly teamed up again with Dru Doescher Stellar (the American Civil Liberties Union activist) for the Children's Variety Network fundraiser.

Appearing at events promoting horse racing and community goodwill, was honorable and her priority. Webb and Fagan preferred that she take paid appearances for their cut. She was unaware that Webb took bribes to enter her on *any* horse; that gave him personal pocket change right off the top.

Revenue from appearances cost Barbara Jo more than they were worth, 50% off the top went to Webb, and he divvied that sum with Fagan. The men made these rules, and she was bound by contract.

Any time off the track caused her to miss work outs, and she suffered the consequences when she hit a losing streak of five consecutive races without coming in the money. Dividing focus (and time) between appearances and racing became a problem the young woman was not prepared for.

Riding races was vital to achieving her journeyman's jockey title, so she persevered through the distraction of the fame factor to reach her personal goal.

Spring racing season was coming, and Kentucky Derby entries were underway. The owner of the stakes horse, Picnic Fair, chose Barbara Jo as the derby jockey. However, Picnic Fair went lame and was scratched from the race.

Diane Crump became the first woman to ride a Triple Crown race in the 1970 Kentucky Derby. The next lady jockey to ride a Triple Crown race was Patricia J. Cooksey in the 1984 Preakness. The illustrious entry of a lady jock for the popular trilogy of racing slowly grew to six women by 2013. Most notable are Julie Krone, who won the 1993 Belmont Stakes, and Rosie Napravnik, who became the highest-placing female jockey finishing fifth in the 2013 Kentucky Derby.

Barbara Jo made a Canadian weekend racing debut at Assiniboia Downs, Winnipeg. The track owner paid for her appearance. The Assiniboia racing crowd was large and enthusiastic. On Friday, she ran first in one of three races. Assiniboia racing program promoted and highlighted her.

Welcome, Barbara Jo Rubin!

Assiniboia Downs is pleased to welcome Barbara Jo Rubin, the first girl jockey to win a race on a recognized racetrack in the United States. Miss Rubin, who has ridden at nine other tracks, chalked up her 16th win Friday when she won on Maureen Deb in the first race. Still embarking on her career as a jockey, Miss Rubin has ridden 59 races and only 16 of her mounts have failed to bring back part of the purse.

B.J. entered her third Saturday race at Assiniboia Downs, on Deuce of Diamonds and trotted the post parade. The post parade is a barometer of how the horse feels and acts minutes up to the race and can also be a jockey's first time on the horse.

Diamond Deuce trembled and leaned against the pony horse during the post parade. Barbara Jo felt his fear and trepidation. He dripped with nervous sweat and hesitantly loaded into the starting gate only to bolt through it before the race began.

Barbara Jo's knees slammed into the steel barrier. She ignored the pain, while the gate crew reloaded the entry. In the few moments the rest of the field horses entered their gates; Deuce reared and flipped over. He thrashed and crushed Barbara Jo, until he was pulled out of the gate and told to reload for the third time. Barbara Jo stammered to her feet in a blurry consciousness, remounted, and the race went off.

Deuce ran on frantic fear with Barbara Jo riding on adrenaline. They did not make the purse, but they did finish the race.

She survived her first career injury. Both of her knee meniscus cartilage was torn, and the rest of her body was crushed, battered, and bruised. The knee injuries alone required six to eight weeks off under complete rest. Webb only allowed her two weeks recovery, blatantly disregarding that a jockey needs healthy knees like a racehorse needs healthy legs. The insufficient recuperation caused a downward spiral of dismal outcome.

History wasn't finished with Barbara Jo Rubin. Soon she would become the first of her kind to retire at twenty years old.

Chapter 5

Fall to Pieces

*"In life you have three choices;
give in, give up or give it all you got."*
- Charleston Parker, author

The dream to be a jockey had become reality. The responsibility to sustain that livelihood also included the pressure to endure its wear and tear. Barbara Jo was tough and could manage her career choice but was defenseless in the war of greed and would be a casualty in that battle.

Webb insisted for Barbara Jo to continue racing while injured, with a non-diplomatic pressure that left no room for negotiation, and he punctuated his persuasion with a footnote of *make hay while the sun shines* theory.

He coldly explained, "You're a new face and you can't let them forget you. It's best to cash in while this lasts"

Barbara Jo gave in to the intimidation that you don't bite the hand that feeds you. The contract with Webb kept her dream alive despite killing her physically, emotionally and financially. This was her dream regardless of the downside.

The percentage of a race's total purse during 1969 was only awarded to the four highest finishers. The purse money was allotted 65% to the winner, 20% to the second-place finisher, 10% to the third, and 5% to the fourth. This distribution had flaws and often entries scratched from a race decreasing the field. The Florida racing association responded to low race entries by extending the purse. By 1975, Florida awarded 1% of the purse money to *all* horses in a race finishing lower than fourth, guaranteeing that an owner wouldn't lose money by entering a race. Other states soon followed Florida's initiative.

As the trainer, Webb made 10% of a winning purse. As the jockey, Barbara Jo earned a 10% share of the trainer's take and was obligated to pay her agent and valets fees, totaling another 25% cut out of her 10% take.

She was also responsible for paying taxes on her income. While under contract with Webb, she could not ride other horses, unless he agreed. Barbara Jo gave a lot for others to take. But freedom awaited, if she could ride it out until her journeyman status. It was a system just shy of The Hunger Games.

A horse racing jockey is a dangerous profession and like any competitive sport, it has some participants that cheat and sabotage the competition. B.J. holds true to the fact of not squealing about infractions against her, since a winning female was enough controversy without making more attention.

Before video cameras were installed on horse racetracks, patrol judges sat in bird nests with binoculars to observe the field from upper vantage points where charges would be called on riders guilty of bad behavior.

Seasoned jockeys knew the blind spots of the bird nests at each track and could get away with boxing a horse in to slow it down or whipping another rider with their crop without being caught.

If a crew member of the starting gate stood on the pontoon plate and held your horse's bridle saying, "Don't even think about winning this race". You still wouldn't tattle.

You could, however, win anyway.

Many times, Barbara Jo was asked, "Why do you want to be a jockey?"

Barbara Jo's answer was simple, "To win."

"I'm not a suffragette or female militant or anything like that. I always thought of myself as sort of ugly. I guess I'm trying to prove myself the only way I know how, by riding horses. I've always loved to ride. If I get killed now at least I'm enjoying myself."

Two weeks after her serious injury, Barbara Jo debuted at Liberty Bell Park Racetrack, Philadelphia, for the summer meet. Her knees were a far cry from recovering but regardless she trained and raced. She worked in acute pain and wrapped her swollen knees for riding.

She earned two wins and two second place finishes but under the continual stress her knees worsened. She had worn through her tenacity and asked Webb to show mercy and give her recovery time.

"I just don't think my knees will ever get better if I don't give them some real time off. The swelling even makes it hard for me to ride in position."

Webb retorted, "You're doing fine, don't stop now. We've got a whole lot of summer races set up here. He shared an idea, "But if you're so bothered by some aches, use pain killers to work through it. Hell, everybody uses them. You're young and you'll mend," he concluded.

He supplied pain medication which masked the intense pain, but she was fighting a losing battle.

On June 21, Barbara Jo ran her second race of the day on, Restforall. During the race, Restforall clipped another horse's heels, tripped, fell and rolled along the track. She sustained a concussion, bruises, and stitches. She also received her first (and only) racing violation. The stewards called it a careless riding offense, suspending her off the track for five days.

Time off put weight on the scale, so Webb advised a pharmaceutical answer for that, too.

"These will make it a lot easier, and you won't have to worry. They'll burn off weight while you're sitting around,"

The amphetamines didn't work fast enough for rapid weight loss, so Barbara Jo purged after meals. Nobody noticed her mental and physical deterioration, except Gordie Gubin, who didn't know what he saw but knew that it wasn't right.

Gubin was on leave from the Navy that summer in Philadelphia, and he visited Liberty Bell Park. Gubin could not forget the unforgettable, Barbara Jo.

Gubin perched at the winner's circle at Liberty Park and bet on the nose for her, but she didn't make the board. He watched her second race but again she didn't place. Spectators noticed the handsome fellow, dressed in his Navy whites carrying flowers sitting nervously in the grandstand thinking, *third time's a charm,* waiting for her final race of the night.

Barbara Jo's throbbing knees and medicated mind prevented her personal best. She finished her last race, exhausted and burnt out. Barbara Jo dismounted, weighed out and headed for her dressing room to leave. Her races at Liberty Bell Park Racetrack were fulfilled and she was scheduled next for racing in Venezuela.

As she swung open the exit door into the starry summer night, the racetrack dirt lingered in the air. She wiped away dirty grime from her eyes then heard a familiar voice.

"Hey Barbara Jo!" Gordie yelled out.

Gordie watched Barbara Jo approach him with a weak smile. He stepped forward to give her a hug.

She leaned into his embrace," What brings you out here?" Gordie played it cool and said, "I'm on leave out here and figured I'd check in on you."

Another familiar voice called out, "Hey, there stranger!"

Barbara Jo's sister, Francine, walked up. Francine spent the summer working at Liberty Bell Park as a track laundry assistant, and the sisters lived together. Francine was meeting up with Barbara Jo for a ride back to the apartment.

Gordie laughed, "Well, I get to see both you girls? This is my lucky night!"

Francine was more animated than her sister with smiles and questions. Barbara Jo limped as they walked and talked together through the parking lot.

Concern crossed Gordie's mind and although Barbara Jo wasn't in Venezuela yet, she was indeed, a thousand miles away. He wanted to ask the girls out for dinner to enjoy their company. He wanted to know how Barbara Jo was really doing but didn't. Gordie heard his dad's voice reminding him that *gentlemen don't force their way into a woman's heart.*

Barbara Jo reached for the keys of her new blue 1969 Mustang, a gift from Charles Town track after her historic victory in February.

Standing at the car, Gordie concluded, "Well, I guess you ladies have an early morning. It's so good to see you both again and I'm glad I got to catch you for a hello. You take care now."

With a slight hesitation, Barbara Jo answered, "Ok." and whispered into his ear, "You take care, too, Gordie".

Francine hugged Gordie, pulling away to look at him and say, "It's always good to see you."

Gordie closed Barbara Jo's car door and waved as she drove off. There was finality; his hopeful possibility for romance blew away like the dust flying off the Mustang's tires.

While driving away Francine said," Good seeing Gordie, wasn't it?"

"Oh yeah, it sure is," Barbara Jo nodded and moved Gordie's flowers on the front seat as she fumbled for her purse. She grimaced as she swallowed a couple of pain pills.

Pain is the body's signal of distress meant to cause attention. Barbara Jo's athletic mentality of mind-over-matter released endorphins with beneficial results, and her conditioned physique tolerated most demands. But now, her physical deterioration was at an overwhelming level, and weight limit stress was just as intense as her physical injuries.

Jockeys widely use solutions to shave pounds off such as purging food, overuse of laxatives, diuretics, and sweating in racetrack sauna rooms.

A woman jockey was not allowed access to the track saunas (hot boxes) like the male jockeys. So, she came up with her own method to sweat off weight like the boys. She blasted her car heater on high, kept the windows rolled up, wore a long sleeve sweatshirt and sweatpants over her body that she covered in plastic wrap.

The technique basted her like a turkey creating the same effect of a 105-degree sauna. A human's electrolyte balance is severely altered by sweating like this, especially when done regularly and especially with minimum caloric intake.

Charles Town upgraded their jockey quarters in 1972, at the price tag of $100,000 to include separate gender dressing rooms and hot boxes for ladies.

Calder Race Track followed with appropriate upgrades, too, and the trend soon spread across the country. Time eventually made the playing field equal, just not in time for her.

She speculated whether her career injuries compounded any residual effects of her polio impediment, and she dug deeper into her resilience to regain her well-being. Before racing next in Venezuela, she stopped taking pain medication and amphetamines cold turkey.

Races in Caracas, Venezuela were held at the elegant La Rinconada. The racetrack opened in 1959 and was designed by the American architect, Arthur Froehlich (the designer of Aqueduct track in New York City). La Rinconada's racecourse hippodrome was nestled in a lush valley, decorated with Italian murals and a coliseum seating capacity of eight thousand. It was a grand venue for horse racing.

The Venezuelan races were the first time Barbara Jo shared the program with another woman jockey. Twenty-one-year-old

American, Diane Crump made her debut at La Rinconada during this time, too.

The women did not compete against each other and met briefly in the racetrack dressing room. Together these agents of change, shared a glimpse of the near future, where women were given the same but separate amenities.

Diane Crump's trainer, Don Divine, was also her husband at the time. Barbara Jo noticed that a supportive business partnership was instrumental in sustaining a long-term career. La Republics newspaper covered the pair's performance reporting that even if they didn't win - they looked great.

These two trailblazers along with all the other women during the late 1960's and early 1970's, changed the future of gender equality through their profession of horse racing.

At the beginning of gender integration, racetracks called an all-female field of competitors, Powder Puff Derbies. Mixed gender jockey horse races in the 70's were promoted as Jack & Jill races. Novelty named races faded away when both male and female jockeys became the norm.

Chapter 6

Out to Pasture

*You must always know how long
to stay and when to go.*
-The Chicks

Timing is important in horse racing. Jockeys master the mental ability to clock horses' speed. Barbara Jo achieved all the essential racing elements but was stuttering with her health and sanity. Her knees might never be the same after the Canadian race injuries and recent sobriety gave her clarity to realize the reality of limitations.

She ran on the Maryland racing circuit which had a flare for celebrating fall festivals August through September. The tracks held carnival festivities of games, food stands and rides. The venues packed spectators who were thrilled to see her race. Despite the fanfare and performing well, privately her stability was waning.

In a two-week period of training, Barbara Jo went off horses fourteen times and sustained broken bones (fingers, toes, ribs, tailbone), stitches and concussions. The end of Barbara Jo's apprentice jockey career was caused by accumulated injuries in a quick period, with one specific day being the last straw.

Galloping a horse on the track before sunrise is called daylighting. Webb stood at the rail clocking her work out on the Pimlico track. Senses are heightened in daylighting, and Barbara Jo's vision adjusted to the inky dark blue light as the awakening sounds of the morning amplified.

The serenity of the horse's breathing and his rhythmic pace was all beautifully normal, until she heard the tragic pop of the horse's leg bone snap, and she was thrown off.

She landed safely, but the horse did not. He rolled along the track, groaning from shock and pain. When the majestic athlete thrashed and convulsed, his shattered bones rattled like a bag of marbles.

Another rider and galloping horse were quickly coming up on the accident on the dim morning track. Barbara Jo ran over to her injured companion and stood over the horse shouting, "DOWN ON THE RAIL!" to prevent collision.

After the rider pulled up, Barbara Jo bent down to the injured horse and cradled his head. The track ambulance quickly came to aid. The vet and barn grooms grimly knew the outcome.

The ambulance driver asked Barbara Jo, "Are you okay?"

She couldn't respond.

Echoing sounds of the horse's leg bone popping throbbed in her ears. She was escorted away as the suffering horse was euthanized on the track.

The deep imprint of his body in the dirt was tilled over by a tractor before the next round of workouts. Barbara Jo's firsthand experience of a horse's fatal injury on the track was heartbreaking.

Webb met up with Barbara Jo at the track medical office and extended his hand holding her helmet out and said, "The day's not over see you at the barn".

The sun was up, and her next horse waited. Reely Beeg, pranced about full of piss and vinegar and was literally chomping at his bit. A groom gave her a leg up into the saddle and while trotting to the track, she repeated the mantra, *mind over matter.*

She felt the familiarity of Reely Beeg's hulking obstinance. Stepping onto the track, she jogged him toward Webb for instructions. Reely Beeg could be mean, but at this moment, he was abominable.

Propping is a racetrack term for a horse that digs its front feet into the ground to stop suddenly. Reely Beeg's propping maneuver also included a shoulder drop, guaranteed to throw off *any* rider. She went off the horse, right in front of the trainers at the rail.

As Barbara Jo stood up from her dirt bath, Reely Beeg played keep away from being retrieved. Purely frustrated, she threw a dirt clod at Reely Beeg, hitting him in the neck and driving him away in an angry gallop. As the trainers watched, they expressed a range of laughter and snickers.

"THAT'S IT!" Barbara Jo shouted, holding back hysteria she continued, "I'm taking a break…I NEED a break".

She walked off and away from the track.

The rookie had launched an explosive blast of 98 career starts with 49 wins on sixteen different racetracks within eight months. She pulled the plug.

Just a week earlier, she raced at Charles Town riding on the beloved Cohesion for the last time. They placed fourth, but something within Barbara Jo was breaking down.

"If I had known that was our last ride, I would have said goodbye", she mentions now.

Barbara Jo went home to Country Club Ranches in Florida and rested. She indulged in horse riding for daily pleasure. She healed up the assorted physical breaks and mental aches and gained back a normal weight of one hundred and twenty pounds.

Maxine was elated to have her daughter home. Barbara Jo's dad hatched an idea to open a bar in the Aztec Hotel called The Winner's Circle. It was clearly aimed for the racing crowd near Gulfstream Racetrack and clearly meant to capitalize on his daughter's fame. Barbara Jo didn't allow the use of her likeness or name in any of his business ventures.

Her self-imposed time off paralleled remedy for fatigued and burnt-out horses. When astute owners or trainers recognize exhaustion in a horse, they put the horse on stall rest or (even better) pasture time and include no demands to revive the body and spirit. The horse remembers what it's like to just be a horse. The time necessary for healing is hard to forecast but when the time is right, there is often productivity again.

When Barbara Jo's time was right, she dropped to her racing weight of 106 pounds. Resting for five months brought back her well-being and motivation. The vapor trail of her dream still existed, and she resumed Webb's contract.

He had horses waiting at Tropical Park to gallop and train, always his priority. Her jockey career was inconsequential to him, and in fact, it was a nuisance. This time there was not any tug of war over personal ambitions; winning came first, plain and simple.

Many horse trainers are of the opinion that a good exercise rider is harder to find than a great jockey. Barbara Jo's comeback progressed well. She worked as hard as ever to get herself and the horses ready for spring racing.

When a stirrup slips out from a loose or faulty safety clip, it hinders the workout, so wrapping a strand of wire to the saddle breakaway clip prevents losing the stirrup. Consequently, a wired stirrup is a dangerous practice that puts the rider at a grave risk. Barbara Jo's stirrups were wired on this tragic day.

The horse galloped on the track normally until he swayed and bolted sideways into the inside rail. The force threw her offside leg out of its stirrup, and she swung off the horse's back with her other leg caught up in the wired stirrup. She was dragged along the rail until the wire finally broke.

Barbara Jo tumbled to the ground like a pair of casino dice and miraculously, stood up and walked off the track. Battered by the trauma, she went home for the day. Injuries can be invisible while adrenaline and endorphins are doing their job.

At home a throbbing excruciating pain ran through her left thigh. The accident caused severe damage to her femoral artery that formed a blood clot, proving disastrous. She had a dismal hospital stay.

Doctors confronted Barbara Jo with the somber possibility of leg amputation. The duration of attention and treatment in the hospital saved her leg, but the physician insisted that her occupation as a jockey was over.

She hadn't made it to her pinnacle of success to become a journeyman jockey but counted her blessings for the ability to walk away from being a jockey while she literally, could still walk. Webb dissolved their apprentice contract and all associations with her.

"I wanted to ride longer but ended up having too many falls", she stated graciously, as the official reason for retirement.

She took up the next best option for a professional horsewoman's livelihood and became a racehorse trainer. It was a natural fit, considering all her knowledge of Thoroughbreds and her understanding of the racetrack industry. Women were more prevalent in horse training versus jockeying, but Barbara Jo wasn't concerned with gender restrictions anymore. She no longer had to prove herself.

Hialeah racetrack issued her an assistant trainer's license and quickly a better offer came from trainer, Tom Jolley, for her to become the assistant trainer at Diamond G Farms in Fellsmere, Florida. This position was an ambitious responsibility for training over thirty newbie racers.

Barbara Jo was confident and competent, and her impeccable work ethic brought an impressive result. William Beele, from Diamond G, spoke highly of her, "She's one in a million. You usually don't find a lady from the racetrack, but there one is. I've never heard her swear or get mad about anything. She has the most even temperament of anyone I know."

However, what did get the lady assistant trainer flared up was the unprofessional attention from Mr. Jolley, who would go on a weekend drink fest and drop by Barbara Jo's bachelorette apartment to proclaim affections. His behavior was appalling, and she shut down any interest in the married employer, who played the innocent boss during the workdays.

She hatched a plan that would keep her viably employed but to get the hell away from Jolley. The lucrative horse racing industry in Florida provided plenty of profitable opportunities, and Barbara Jo offered Jolley a business proposition.

"What if I took a dozen of Diamond G's two-year-old Thoroughbreds to the Tampa area to spread the farms' training reputation and drum up more owners?"

Jolley and the farm's Cuban owners liked her innovation The new business plan also put miles of distance between her and Jolley. She re-located to Tampa, obtained her Tampa trainers license and operated the Diamond G extension barn.

During a workout, a filly showed back soreness. As an astute trainer, Barbara Jo saw reasonable cause to advocate for the horse to be scratched from its next race. The filly's owner ignored Barbara Jo's advice, refused to scratch the entry and ran the horse.

The horse tragically broke her back in the race and was euthanized. The jockey also sustained injuries. Barbara Jo quit training for Diamond G immediately after witnessing a bad decision that caused suffering and death to a horse plus disrespected her knowledge and inflicted injury on a fellow jockey. It was too much for her ethical standards.

"I don't know of anyone in the race business that would stand by such a decision that would hurt a horse or a jockey, and I didn't want to be any part of that" she confides.

Barbara Jo moved on to a new track in Miami. Calder Race Course was an impressive twenty-million-dollar facility on two hundred and twenty acres with an eight-story glass grandstand.

Summer meets could seat a crowd of six thousand and stable twelve hundred horses.

She became a Calder Girl. The Calder Girls mingle with fans during the live races helping the patrons make bets, answer racing questions and other general information. The quick hire paid her rent. Calder Girls happened to be attractive ladies, and she fit that bill, as well.

In public, wearing the Calder Girl uniform of hot pants and white go-go boots, Barbara Jo was recognized by fans and that got too personal. Between heartfelt accolades over her racing days, she would also be asked, *"Whatever happened to you?" "Didn't you used to be...?"*

Those questions rubbed salt in her retired wounds and the sting of missing the race from the top of a horse made her melancholy. She even took up the family habit of gambling to fill the thrill of jockeying. Sometimes she won, sometimes she didn't. Either way, she felt bad.

Being a pedestrian at the racetrack wasn't right. She yearned to earn a living on the back of a horse. Sometimes, passion can mimic addiction, and either way, it is hard to deny its hold.

Case in point, Tony McCoy, a world-famous steeplechase jockey, attests that his career is an addiction. The 2015 documentary film, Being AP, is about McCoy approaching retirement.

The story tells of the decision to stop doing what you're born to do. When the Northern Irish 5"10' steeplechase jockey retired at age 41, he had won nearly every grand competition, held three Guinness World Records but still didn't want to stop riding. Neither did Barbara Jo.

She got back in the saddle again after meeting Eddie Plesa, Sr., a reputable horse trainer aware of her talent. He convinced her to work for him. She ignored her medical directive and rode.

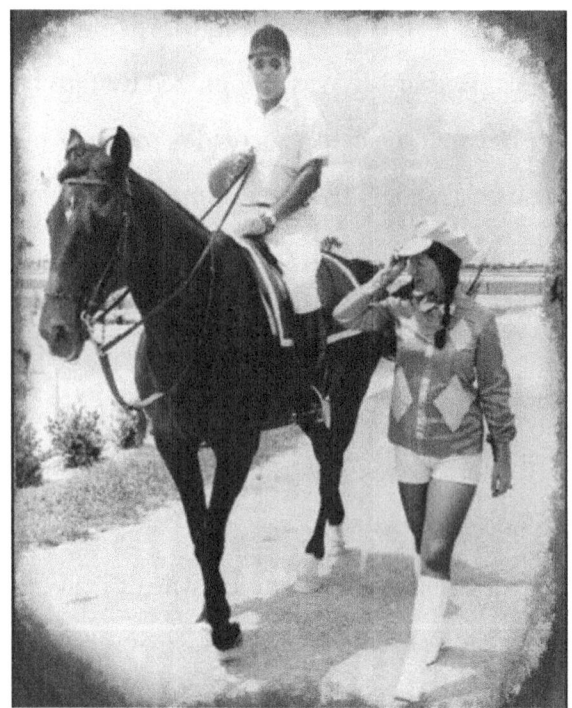

Barbara Jo Rubin at Caulder Race Course

Barbara Jo double-dutied as a gallop lady in the morning and Calder Girl in the afternoon. Word traveled fast on her gun for hire status, and more trainers paid her respectfully as a free agent exercise rider. Within no time, she hung up the go-go boots.

Plesa Sr. was happy with her work. His son, Eddie Plesa, Jr., was just happy with the young lady. Barbara Jo and Jr. were the same age. He drove a red corvette and pursued her romantically. They went from dating to engagement at record speed. In hindsight, she recalls, "Some things can look too good to be true".

Barbara Jo broke off the relationship during the engagement. That didn't go well. The suitor stalked her; wherever she went and often breeched her privacy showing up at her home uninvited. There was an ugly argument where Barbara Jo clearly told him to get lost. He left that day, but the incident had a cataclysmic effect.

She was still simmering with anger from the ferocious fight and saddled up to work on a fresh colt. When she yanked the reins too hard, the horse reared and fell over crushing her pelvis in three places.

She convalesced at home in a full body cast nearly immobile, when Jr. still came by (uninvited) and proclaimed contrite sediments. Just about the time she was healed and about to have her full body cast removed he broke into the house one night and raped her.

"You'll never get away from me", that was all he said.

But she did.

Chapter 7

Finding Another Path

*To the gypsy that remains who faces freedom
with a little fear.*
– Stevie Nicks

The social consciousness of equality among the genders became a growing ideology in the United States. By 1972, Helen Reddy's hit song, I am Woman, played in heavy rotation on commercial radio. The 1973 tennis match between Bobby Riggs and Billie Jean King aka The Battle of the Sexes, was a televised phenomenon as King annihilated Riggs.

Madison Avenue admen hit with campaigns for Virginia Slim cigarettes with the catch phrase, You've Come a Long Way, Baby. Activism for gender equality was labeled Woman's Lib, and it raised convictions and controversy.

The principles of equality didn't fit well with the masses yet. The idea seemed to hang on the country like an over-sized sports coat. Equality calls for liberties to those who need it but often threatens those that are asked to share it.

Barbara Jo abandoned such a war. The experiences of man against woman were far too personal. In the current times, sexual assault, date rape and domestic abuse were rarely open topics. A (hashtag) #timesup movement didn't circulate on social media platforms.

Deep ignorance about rape persecuted the victim not the perpetrator, diminishing the severity of the crime. Those who commit rape have been profiled with the objective to exert power or control. It is an act of aggression, and it is not consensual.

Barbara Jo left her home, horses, and career; all things of comfort to her. She left the limelight that included innuendos, scandals, and scrutinizing judgments. She took a road trip of solitude mixed with hope when she left Florida this time. On one hand, freedom produced inspiration to make a fresh start but on the other hand, leaving home was a lonely prospect.

A nomadic journey is kindred to the American Mustang. In our modern world, Mustangs are driven from their natural life by human advantage. Mustangs are trapped and converted to a life outside their wild natural spirit. They survive being transplanted but not without emotional scars.

History tells the story of Velma Bronn Johnston. A hard-core dedication within her (that lasted twenty-seven years), stepped in to protect the American Mustang in 1950.

In her crusade, Velma crossed paths with a government official who called her Wild Horse Annie, as an insult. Velma embraced the name, since both spirits of Wild West legends; Wild Bill Hickok and Annie Oakley, were appropriate.

Velma suffered from childhood polio in 1917, and her treatment required wearing a cast from waist to the neck for six months. The cast distorted the five-year-old's chin and jaw muscles. Velma confronted life with facial disfigurement.

Raised on a Nevada ranch, as the daughter to an owner-operator of a horse drawn freight liner company, she had learned to dearly love and respect horses.

Wild Horse Annie's persona began when driving down a Nevada highway to her executive secretary job. Velma noticed blood dripping from the back of a trailer truck and followed the trail.

The truck stopped at a pet cannery on the Nevada and California border west of Reno. She watched the tailgate open, to reveal an overloaded compartment of crazed wild Mustangs that had trampled a colt to death during the haul.

A heartfelt compassion led Velma (with the loving support of her husband/rancher, Charlie) to change the inhumane public land management system that allowed extermination of Mustangs from Nevada frontier public grass lands.

Tons of bureaucracy and years of public awareness campaigns later, Velma battled for federal protection of wild horses (and burros). Wild Horse Annie re-branded the wild mustang as an American symbol to be treasured and given a place to exist. Sometimes, things must be viewed differently to better understand their significance.

And now, Barbara Jo was searching for her significance. The open car window blew in a fresh smell of spring, and the delicate lily of the valley blooms awakened memories of happiness as she arrived in College Park, Maryland where she looked up a childhood friend, now a college student at the University of Maryland.

Tom Toms was glad to hear from his buddy Barbara Jo and eager to meet up. He showed her around, and they comfortably fell into their youthful camaraderie. Toms invited Barbara Jo to stay with him. It was no free ride; B.J. found a job as a bartender at a local pub to help pay rent. For the first time in her life, she worked in an environment without horses.

Toms had his future safely planned. He would finish his agriculture degree and operate the family dairy farm in Florida. Barbara Jo spent months contemplating her future and just couldn't see it without horses.

Horses were an extension of herself as real as any other part of her body. It was the blood in her veins. She didn't just like to ride – she needed to ride. Horse riding was where the air and the earth met, where the wind lifted her up to God.

The college town was populated with students and locals who knew nothing of her past profession as a jockey. This new lifestyle was safe but stale. B.J. was restless as a bartender and hated the clientele.

The migratory lifestyle of following race meets was a familiar calling that she had to answer. She headed back to the racetrack circuit for summer racing in Rockingham Park, New Hampshire. She worked as an outrider. These horseback chaperones escort racers in the post parade, catch runaway horses and aid as necessary anywhere on the track or backside.

She was good at playing it safely and helping others, however being close to what you want can ground you or make one sad because it's an imitation of the real thing.

In Miami Beach, during the 1970's, the culture on Collins Avenue was a Mecca of prestige, glamour, wealth and celebrities. Gordie Gubin was out of the Navy and worked as an assistant head doorman at the Playboy Park Plaza. The job required responsibility, energy, and sound mindedness. Gordie took care of business very well.

Alot of vacationers loyally returned to Miami Beach for the summer. A Midwest family (coincidentally named Rubin) was that type and although they had no relation to Gordie's hometown Rubin family, they were familiar friends when residing at the Hotel Deauville.

Gordie and the daughter, Cindy (from St. Louis) fostered a mutual romantic interest. Their courtship led to a fall marriage in 1974. This version of a Gubin/Rubin matrimony made their home in Missouri.

The east coast lost its appeal, for Barbara Jo after a few months, and she left New Hampshire to return home. Francine had told her sister about Gordie marrying and moving away. Barbara Jo felt a biological nudge to start a family of her own. and began to contemplate her life beyond the racetrack.

Tom Toms accomplished his post-graduation plan of managing the family dairy farm in Moore Haven, Florida. When he heard that B.J. was home and off the racetrack, he offered her a job at the dairy farm.

She was treated like a member of the family at the dairy farm and was especially fond of Grandpa Toms. So much so, that the patriarch declared a wish upon his death bed that his grandson marry Barbara Jo. And so, it was done. Surrounded by family and friends, most notably, her mom, Maxine (divorced from Bob) and Grandma Nina (widowed from Clarence), the couple were married December 28, 1975.

Toms was a short athletic man, a wrestler in high school and college who kept up his strong physique, giving him a bit of a Napoleon complex. He was Methodist and did not drink, smoke, or gamble. Toms was a serious and practical guy, an all-work-and-no-play type. Barbara Jo loyally began her wifely duties. It was all very respectable, but it wasn't romantic.

Life on the dairy farm was reclusive. She was lonely with Tom but held the romantic notion that cordial friendship might lead to a passionate relationship. Tom's stoic and cold tendencies hit a record high when B.J. wound up pregnant.

The 1970's gave historic reproduction options to women, popularizing use of The Pill. The hormonal-based contraceptive specified however, that it was not safely recommended for women prone to blood clots. Barbara Jo was susceptible to blood clots; therefore, she couldn't use The Pill.

The United States legalized abortions in 1972, allowing broader reproductive rights for women but Barbara Jo's mate mandated this option as *his* choice. Toms was adamantly opposed to having kids and gave Barbara Jo an agonizing ultimatum to leave if that is what you want.

Staying in the marriage meant that she lost herself in heartache. Despite pleas and attempts to change her husband's mind, he wouldn't give in. They divorced in 1977, and she left with only her Appaloosa (named Biggie) and a trailer.

"If it wasn't for Biggie…well, he gave me something that got me through my depression", she recalls.

A horse/human relationship can make a difference. Often in those instances, horses create healing by their presence of empathy, lack of judgment and unconditional love.

Riding on their backs, the world is seen from a higher level. When trusting a horse to carry us, the sensation generates a metaphysical movement that conveys a therapeutic perception of being transported through obstacles and difficulty.

Horse assisted therapy is an ever-growing field. Equine therapy is not only for physical rehabilitation known as hippotherapy, but there are also equine programs for emotional and behavioral applications. Partnership with a horse, either in groundwork or riding, assists in overcoming or lessening symptoms of depression, addictions, fear and anxieties.

Accredited equine facilitated therapy can aid those with autism and PTSD (post-traumatic stress disorder). Organizations such as, Man-O-War Project, specifically helps veterans for PTSD after combat service and the model has significant benefits.

The highly intuitive nature of the horse provides a healing aspect for humans on multifaceted levels, and Barbara Jo lifted out of deep depression from her divorce with new hope of getting back to life.

She rode Biggie to nearby Florida farms for work and found a job exercising horses at the distinguished Grosse Pointe Stud Farm. Just over thirty years old B.J., was cautious but honestly thrilled to be gainfully employed galloping horses again.

On a routine tack up in the barn, she saw a large lump on the side of the Thoroughbred's neck. The horse also acted peculiarly. She told the trainer that something was wrong.

"Ah, I just wormed him, that's all", he answered and downplayed her insight.

Horses are seasonally de-wormed to prevent parasites. The worming formula was admitted as an injection which caused adverse side effects.

Barbara Jo rode onto the training track where the horse lost consciousness and flipped over the inside rail. There was no time to get off his back, and she suffered a punctured lung that put her in the hospital

Grosse Pointe's employee insurance helped offset medical bills, but her out of pocket costs were substantial. She took the laundry duty job at the farm for income and after six weeks returned to galloping work.

Then it happened again, when another horse had an unusual lump on its neck. B.J. voiced her concern to the trainer, who defiantly stated, "Just gallop my horse for me or leave!"

She left on a stretcher.

Debt and fear of losing the job put her back in the saddle where again the wormer shot caused the horse to faint. She hit the ground hard, and the horse rolled over her. Barbara Jo laid motionless with a dreadful tingling in her hands and feet. Her neck was broken in two places.

She faced unemployment again and after recuperating, searched the newspaper help wanted section and found an ad for a horse carriage trainer at Wycombe House Stud Farm in nearby Reddick, Florida.

The fabulous estate was owned and operated by a wealthy and avid horseman, Philip B. Hofmann. He curated a public carriage museum on the property and competed in carriage driving. Barbara Jo met Hofmann at his museum office among dozens of European and American antique coaches and carriages. Hofmann was especially proud of his Catherine the Great Queen sleigh, acquired from an auction house that traced its origins to the Alfred Gwynne Vanderbilt estate.

The museum at the Wycombe House Stud Farm had an uncanny atmosphere, claimed to be haunted. During their meeting, Philip pointed out that he was familiar with and impressed by her jockey career.

Hofmann, a retired Chairman and CEO of the Johnson & Johnson Company, kept avidly engaged with his equine passion. He was integral to the world class of sport and etiquette of carriage driving. Hofmann and his good friend, Prince Philip, the Duke of Edinburgh, standardized international rules and regulations for the Combined Driving World Championships.

As she sat in an over-stuffed Italian leather chair listening to Hofmann's career and talking about her own, and they made friends quickly. Philip resembled Winston Churchill and while smoking a cigar, wearing a lovable derby hat, Mr. Hofmann confided that his Hosteiner horses were too much for him to train now, at seventy-three years old.

Philip was a well experienced horseman but promised his wife to play it safer in his horse sport. His horses required impeccable skills for the prestigious shows that he entered. Therefore, Hofmann placed the ad for a capable hand to work for his team. Barbara Jo had zero experience in combined carriage driving, but she questioned Philip further about the job requirements. Warmbloods, like the Hosteiner, are bred with the hot-blooded distinction of a Thoroughbred or Arabian horse and a cold-blooded lineage of a heavy work horse such as a Belgian, Shire, or Clydesdale. The bloodline develops a calm, tempered middleweight athletic equine; strong enough to pull a carriage and nimble enough to maneuver obstacles.

Hofmann's Hosteiners were intelligent and capable at their job, but a new Hosteiner on the team was acting up. If he found a suitable trainer to help the new horse, Hofmann would enjoy more competitions and showing events.

"I haven't ever done carriage driving before", Barbara Jo honestly told Hofmann. She had worked with a pair of draft horses at Pleasant Mound that she explained to Hofmann as, "harnessing drafts to wagons".

Philip quickly pointed out, "These are not wagons".

Barbara Jo took note and then propositioned, "If you give me two weeks, I'll figure it out and be ready to work for you".

Hofmann loved her candor and gave her the two weeks to show him what she could do.

"If it looks good, then we'll talk about salary", Philip said. Barbara Jo left their meeting with a handshake and a smile.

A team of carriage horses must operate as combined power - a single unit. Never too old to learn something new, especially about horses, Barbara Jo studied instructional carriage driving books that were part of the museum. Among said rumors of ghosts, B.J. made peace with her own hauntings of horse racing and entered another equine vocation with the same enthusiasm as being a jockey.

Quickly learning all the specialized equipment, (over thirty individual pieces of tack including the carriage, horse collars, girths, surcingles, cruppers, terrets, bridles, reins, whips and bits), Barbara Jo hitched up her Biggie to the wayward Hosteiner and started groundwork.

Reliable (and sensible) Biggie played Zen master to the difficult Holsteiner named Zeezo, With time to spare, Zeezo was introduced to his carriage driving team for Philip's return.

Hofmann stepped into the courtyard of the estate, reviewing his horse team harnessed to his carriage. Barbara Jo handed Philip the reins to his coach. Philip lit a cigar, climbed into the carriage seat and said, "Come with me and let's take a ride".

Aboard and beside the burly driver, Philip tilted the driving whip, motioned the reins and not a word was spoken for the next two hours. He drove the grounds of his entire estate, singing, laughing, and sometimes driving one-handed. He was exuberant, "That's the most fun I've had with my horses in two years!" Barbara Jo's gainful years of employment with Philip B. Hofmann began on the spot. However, time with Hofmann at the Wycombe estate went too fast but not without an incredible adventure first.

Barbara Jo Rubin behind Philip B. Hofmann

Hofmann's legacy essentially created the sport of Combined Driving in the United States. His steadfast friendships with England's royalty led to a special invitation from the Queen to attend and participate in the 1986 Windsor Horse Show. Naturally, Hofmann included his right-hand, Barbara Jo, for the competition in Europe. They traveled to the Windsor show where Barbara Jo was unexpectedly put on the spot. In England, Philip suffered a mild heart attack and was scratched from the show. Hofmann was determined for his team to represent and requested Barbara Jo to drive.

The rules of the Windsor Horse Show require high-level competitors of national championship status. Barbara Jo had never participated in any driving competition, but Philip called Queen Elizabeth to ask favor in this situation. By special permission of Queen Elizabeth, Barbara Jo was allowed to enter the Windsor Horse Show.

Comparable to Olympic equestrian eventing, the sport of combined driving comprises three disciplines; dressage, cross-country marathon and obstacle cone driving. Barbara Jo competed in the FEI (Federation Equestre International) event for the United States and placed in the pairs division and won a presentation award in pairs combined driving.

After the Windsor show, Hofmann remained healthy up until a casual pleasure carriage drive that ended in tragedy.

Each position of a four-in-hand horse carriage team has a specific role. The front lead pair work as the power steering. Wheelers are hitched closest to the carriage behind the lead pair, pulling the weight of the carriage. They work like the dually tires of a pickup truck.

On Philip's last carriage ride, the team's left wheeler swished his tail and wrapped it in the carriage wheel. Hofmann stopped down allowing Barbara Jo (riding at his side) to lend assistance. The wheeler horse reared and bucked, setting off an agitated chain reaction in the team that caused Hofmann to drop the carriage reins. The team took off in a runaway gallop toward a narrow-fenced lane. Hofmann pulled the carriage brake abruptly, and the sudden stop threw the coach off balance, flipping into the fence.

Hofmann's ribs were broken and while in the Miami Beach hospital, he developed pneumonia and died at the age of seventy-seven.

Barbara Jo dearly missed Mr. Hofmann, and the job at Wycombe Stud Farm wasn't the same without him. His loyal and respectful character gave Barbara Jo the sense of a real father. Hofmann's widow quickly liquidated the estates' assets, which included Barbara Jo.

B.J. left Wycombe Farm but not empty-handed; she had world class credentials. All that had been accomplished wasn't taken away. Prior to his death, Philip had given Barbara Jo a carriage, tack and a trailer and she moonlighted in her own part-time carriage business. Classic Carriages was now her sole livelihood, and she was her own boss.

Classic Carriages catered to weddings and special occasions. The customers loved the beautiful driver who wore full carriage driving regalia; a black tail driving jacket, top hat, and white gloves. Biggie (aka Mr. Big) was groomed in braids, donning black leather and polished silver tack as he pulled a traditional vis-a-vis (face to face) two seated silver carriage with burgundy wool seats. Barbara Jo gave off a sense of royalty and class. She was the queen of her survival in the reality of adversity.

Chapter 8

Making the Best of It

Never love anyone who treats you like you're ordinary.

– Oscar Wilde, poet

Barbara Jo ran into a familiar fellow at a Classic Carriage business event in Ocala; although it took a few moments to recognize him. The six-foot, rugged desperado had a chiseled gristle about him from his share of doing life's hard times.

"Oh my gosh, is that you, Dick?"

"Yup. Barbara Jo Rubin, whadda ya know!" Warman joked, "Still working for ice cream?"

"No, I don't do that anymore".

It had been decades since their match racing days together. B.J. only saw the nuances of the young maverick from back then. Dick Warman was now a Miami Elevators repairman working a job in Ocala.

"You still look the same, Barbara Jo. Well, maybe even better now".

She was a gorgeous woman, in her late thirties aging timelessly; strong and slender, favoring the likeness of the raven-haired American country music songbird, June Carter Cash.

The memories of riding in Warman's match races flew throughout B.J.'s thoughts. The exhilaration of her test race that she won riding bareback; was just one of a million lessons she earned to be the jockey she became.

It was easy then. Warman only wanted her to win and had never shown animosity to her talent. Time does an interesting thing to memories; it can make fondness out of compatibility and reality blind to truth.

Dick was only a horseman as a hobby now but invited her to see his five-acre horse farm in Loxahatchee, leveraging their re-acquaintance to pursue more. They began a romance, but it wasn't practical. The distance between them was inconvenient. On July 1, 1988, they were married.

Maxine Rubin attended her daughter's courthouse ceremony. The West Palm Beach newspaper ran a feature about the 1969 celebrity jockey marrying the elder match race trainer who had started Barbara Jo racing as an adolescent.

Barbara Jo Warman ran her Classic Carriage business out of the Warman Farm in Loxahatchee, Florida. It served the affluent West Palm Beach customers, including the emerging township of Wellington, recognized as the "winter equestrian capital of the world". Her talents also double-dutied for the Warman farm by ramping up horse training and lessons.

Warman shared his affinity for mules with his wife, and Barbara Jo found that mules rode slightly differently than horses but were just as fascinating. Mules are the product of breeding the male donkey to a female horse. The strength and surefootedness from the donkey meshed with the beauty, agility, and compatibility to humans, of the horse, creates the worthiest of pack animals - the mule, who are notoriously known for being stubborn. In that department, a mule named Emma took the prize.

Warman bought the paint bay with four white stocking legs and a traditional long mule head with big ears as a bargain, but the ordeal of just bringing her home gave him second thoughts. Emma's front legs were tangled in the trailer's hay net, causing it to shake and shimmy as her bellowing brays roared out. Warman's face was bloody, and he held the pieces of his broken eyeglasses.

"Damn thing kicked me in the head like a sniper! This girl is a hum dinger", he told Barbara Jo as he rubbed his head and walked away.

Barbara Jo trained Emma. But first had to meticulously pry open the mules' mouth with a screwdriver to take a bit. Over time, with consistent care, Emma became a very refined riding mule.

While Barbara Jo managed Warman Farm into a full boarding and training facility that averaged fifty students weekly, Mr. Warman went into retirement from his day job and reacquainted with his old vice of heavy drinking. This put a bad wedge between the couple.

A prospective horse buyer met up with Barbara Jo at the barn interested in a saddle bred horse the farm posted for sale. George Wedgworth introduced himself and negotiated the deal.

He was the CEO for Wedgworth Inc., a family owned and operated Florida sugar cane and agriculture business, legendary for its environmentalist vision and heritage. Wedgworth was the Bill Gates of the worldwide sugar industry. George could have acted like a hoity-toity millionaire but instead was a down-to-earth family man.

He was a tall athletic sixty-seven-year-old, that could pass as a twin to the famous baseball player, Joe DiMaggio. The horse loving gentleman asked to ride the prospective gaited gelding, Goldie, for his granddaughter.

They closed the sale and B.J. trailered Goldie to his home at the large farm property in nearby Yeehaw Junction. The estate was so humongous that it had its own exit ramp off the highway. George offered Barbara Jo the full-time property manager job requiring that Barbara Jo reside on the grounds. She accepted.

While separated from Warman, B.J. ruminated over the bad marriage that her dad created with her mom. She phoned her mom often and noticed a significant mental cloudiness and verbal confusion on the calls. Maxine was examined and diagnosed with the early stages of Alzheimer's disease.

The siblings discussed the care of their mom's condition, and Barbara Jo chose to bring Maxine to live in Florida. A small farmhouse was available in the community of Indian Hammock (close to the Wedgworth estate). B.J. made an offer on her mom's behalf.

In that summer, Fourth of July festivities rolled around with the anticipation of bar-be-ques, ice cold libations and fireworks and in Missouri, Gordie Gubin, (who had divorced in December 1996), counted down the end of the day at his desk making one last business call.

The patriotic holiday prompted thoughts in rapid sequences; his Navy service, the pledge of allegiance "with liberty and justice for all"... liberty... Liberty Park racetrack.... Barbara Jo Rubin. The moment felt like holding a faded valentine.

He roamed through his rolodex for a business number to call but stopped at the r's, landing on Michael Rubin, Barbara Jo's brother. Gordie telephoned Mike for old times' sake. Their conversation melted the miles away, as ageless friendships do. Between the updates and recollections, Mike had a hunch that the inevitable topic of his sister would come up.

Gordie asked, "And how is Barbara Jo? What's she doing these days?".

Mike gave an overview of nothing too personal and offered, "I've got a phone number for her. I'm sure she'd do a better job telling you what she's up to".

Gordie called the number he was given and a raspy voice answered and questioned, "*Who* is this?"

Gordie replied "I'm trying to reach Barbara Jo. This is her friend, Gordie Gubin."

Warman handed the phone to his estranged wife who happened to be at their barn. A short flat conversation came and went before Barbara Jo said goodbye to Gordie. She had to rush out and close the deal to her mom's house. B.J. managed the details of moving her mom from Illinois. When all things were set, she phoned her brother with the final details.

"I'll fly in on Friday afternoon. If you can have the U-Haul all packed and Mom ready, I'll drive out on Saturday afternoon."

Michael took note and added, "Hey, Gordie called me, and we caught up on things. He and Cindy got divorced awhile back. Anyway, I told him about Mom's Alzheimer's and that you were bringing her to Florida. He asked about you, so I just gave him your number – you shoulda heard from him. I think he just wanted to say hi."

"Oh yeah, he called. He seemed good. We didn't talk for long. Hey, do you have his number in St. Louis that you can give me?"

The call began comfortably with the standard protocol, "Hello, Gordie. How you doing?" and then fell into a rhythm of rapport, with laughs and silent smiles.

Barbara Jo initiated to see each other for a quick visit when she came up to Illinois. Gordie's chance of a lifetime knocked, and he flung open the door with. "Hey, how about I just pick you up at the airport?"

"Well, okay. That'd be great! Here's my flight number."

St. Louis, Missouri, hugs the Mississippi River bordering Illinois. Commerce and communities co-exist along the bi-state region, complimenting each other. Outside the city limits, Missouri's terrain gets rocky with Ozark Mountain cliffs peeking out along thick woodlands. Illinois geography is spread out like squares of a quilt with prairies, corn fields, and soybean farms.

She flew into St. Louis Lambert airport and Gordie would taxi Barbara Jo to Mulberry Grove, Illinois, which is just over an hour's ride east over the Mississippi.

Gordie gussied up with a shower, shave and shine like a teenager going to prom, although he reasoned with his fluttering heart, to be realistic. A pleasant reunion and a lift from the airport could be good enough.

Travelers moved past Gordie at the airport as he waited to see Barbara Jo from behind a pillar in the terminal gate. Barbara Jo spotted him in the distance, scoping her out. She flushed with fondness. Gordie's feet floated across the floor to her as she held out her arms. They embraced and kissed. A serious mutual affection took hold where time had never allowed before.

The drive to Mulberry Grove, weaves through the city of St Louis with restaurants and sights, but the rest of the world just didn't exist for Barbara Jo and Gordie. She was romantically attracted to her childhood friend whose full curly dark afro hair had receded to silver and charcoal waves. He was healthy, fit, dynamic as ever and exhilarating company.

Gordie's car idled in the driveway of the house with its air conditioning overloading from the heat of their physical chemistry. This quick reunion counted down like midnight on Cinderella. In a few more hours, Barbara Jo would be trucking back to Florida.

"You've got to stay another day", Gordie pleaded.

Barbara Jo was consolatory, "I really can't. We'll stay in touch, don't worry."

"Barbara Jo, stay another day. One more night...... let me show you how a man is supposed to love a woman".

In the luster of this summer night, it was obvious that the stars were aligned, and Barbara Jo agreed to stay for another night and have a date with Gordie.

Maxine noticed her daughter's radiance on this visit. Maxine's memory connected to the summers her children spent on the farm in Illinois. It gave her serenity knowing that she had given the kids the best life that she could. When Barbara Jo asked to leave a day later for Florida, for an evening with Gordie, Maxine didn't mind.

Gubin made their date a romantic adventure. He knew how to enjoy good things in life and the true value of loved ones. Even to this day, when Gordie and Barbara Jo talk about their first date in 1998 - each giggle and blush.

Barbara Jo settled her mom into the new home in Florida, resumed her work at the Wedgworth estate and filed for divorce from Warman.

Gordie visited Florida during their long-distance courtship. His times with Barbara Jo at the Wedgworth estate were like Shangri-La. Important things became quite clear to Gordie about Barbara Jo; her incredulous work ethic, the mastery of her horse passion and her beauty blooming in love's radiance.

Barbara Jo's plate was full and bountiful. She loved caring for Mom, had a loving relationship with Gordie, and she had a magnificent job.

Gordie wondered, *how could she ever leave this?* His full-time life was back in St. Louis, Missouri. When B.J.'s divorce from Warman was finalized, Gordie proposed and during their engagement, Barbara Jo decided to move to the Midwest to be his wife.

The bridegroom became a man on a mission, searching for the right place for Barbara Jo, which had to include horses. Gordie lined up real estate options in Missouri and Illinois for Barbara Jo to review on a visit.

When they arrived at a property in Troy, Illinois, her heart swelled. Between fields of corn and soybeans down a private rocky driveway lined with pine trees, awaited a sixteen-acre property with a thirty-stall horse barn and an indoor riding arena. Past the barn and alongside a private lake was a ranch house nestled into a grassy hillside. Gordie and Barbara Jo had found their home. She looked into his eyes hesitantly questioning, "You'd buy this for me?"

She had never been given a choice where to live with a man before. Gordie replied in a heartbeat, "If that's what you want, I will".

She named their home, Classic Acres.

Chapter 9

Classically Forever

*I'm going to catch that horse if I can and when I do
I'll give her my brand and we'll be friends for life.*
- *Chestnut Mare,* The Byrds

Gordie and Barbara Jo's love made a passionate future. Their childhood familiarity was sealed by a mutual code of values. Neither was the kind of person that could stay forever with someone who lacked the gumption between right and wrong.

On a basic level, love is having needs met. Barbara Jo self-earned a PHD in horse husbandry with intuitive skills, practicality and devotion. She gave them what they needed; food, shelter, medical attention, occasionally a psychologist and always respect and understanding.

Caring deeply for horses met her need for a purpose that resulted in a fervent livelihood. There's a possibility of such a relationship between horse and human producing oxytocin (the biological love drug). Yet, even in the unconventionality of her life at times, Barbara Jo yearned for trust and safety on a human level with another person.

Life brought her many blessings but not a soul mate or children. Gordie came along giving Barbara Jo a place of honor in both his heart and his children's young adult lives. Gubin loaded up the farm to move Barbara Jo and Maxine from Florida to Illinois. "It was like the Beverly Hillbillies! My gosh, with all the stuff we had to pack and move! I had all of Mom's things, my belongings and carriages, saddles, tack and eight horses."

Head of the herd was her beloved Biggie who would live out his lifetime of twenty-seven years at Classic Acres.

Before the wedding, Barbara Jo made Classic Acres a thriving business filling all the empty stalls with boarders. She acquired lesson students for multiple equestrian disciplines and various levels of skills.

There was a flourishing Thoroughbred community of horse trainers, breeders and riding enthusiasts residing in the bi-state area partly due to Collinsville, Illinois's Fairmount Park racetrack established in 1925. Thoroughbreds were regularly adopted by new owners and retrained for life off the racetrack.

At Classic Acres, Barbara Jo began the discipline of dressage. Dressage combines mental and physical harmony between rider and horse where the grace and strength of the horses' natural movements appear to be dancing with the rider.

After achieving new skills, B.J. competed on her most noteworthy steeds; Isaac, Twilight, Romancer and Ferrari, and won national and regional awards.

"I like the whole-body approach of dressage and the balance of the seat," she explains. "Dressage requires pressure versus force".

In Gordie's opinion, waiting for life with Barbara Jo only meant that the best was yet to come.

"Besides the strong physical attraction, we have so much in common". Gordie explains, "We think alike, do things together. It's magical. I love her good nature, her beauty and her lively spirit." Gordie continues, "She always has my back. I totally trust her".

The couple know the importance of communication but deem respect highest on their list of must haves. Both have equality in the relationship, operating as a team. Gordie maintains. "If one person on the team isn't happy then the team isn't succeeding."

Like minded but not identical, Barbara Jo and Gordie do have differences. Gordie has ridden horses on trail rides but admits that it's not his favorite thing, opting for riding together on a Harley.

Gordie admits that he is not as trusting towards people as his better half and doesn't understand those that have hurt her. "She's tough but has a heart of gold and there's something wrong with you if you take advantage of that", he declares.

He worries about injuries when B.J. takes on difficult horses to train but realizes horses are her family. The couple uphold an open-door policy with family – which included Bob Rubin.

Bob made visits to Classic Acres, later in his life after he was divorced from his second wife. He worked as a security guard at a Florida casino and had done the unimaginable - faced his drinking demon and went sober cold turkey.

No one knew what to expect on Bob's first visit to Classic Acres. Bob came remorseful and apologetic to both Barbara Jo and Maxine.

Barbara Jo reminded Bob daily of his wayward past. Bob listened to her pain and made amends. Bob was welcomed to Classic Acres for subsequent stays.

At seventy-five years old, Bob Rubin died August 31, 2001, of lung cancer. Bob Rubin, who lived like hell, went out like a lamb. The day after her fifty second birthday, Barbara Jo Rubin wed Gordie Gubin, November 22, 2001. The bridal party and entourage of family and friends chartered a bus to the justice of the peace and then dinner in St Louis at The Feasting Fox restaurant for the celebration.

Their marriage grew while the Classic Acre home saw loved ones come and go. Barbara Jo took in Grandma Nina until she passed at ninety-eight years old, in 2002. Five years later Maxine passed on at eighty-two years old. Barbara Jo became the sole matriarch.

Classic Acres barn was hardly an empty nest. It stabled an assortment of Barbara Jo's own horses and mules. Boarders stabled Haflingers, Friesians, Quarter Horses, Mustangs, Shetland ponies, Fox Trotters, Arabians, Gypsy Vanners and good ol' Thoroughbreds.

The boarding owners don't feel like customers. There's a fellowship that unites the personal passion for their horse. Some owners trail ride or show in competitions, but most don't. None has been a jockey, none are judged for their hobby, or expertise level, - all that matters is that you love your horse. Barbara Jo generously gives her knowledge, instruction, and friendship.

Young at heart and still grabbing the gusto of life, Gordie retired in 2009. Travel sparked the couples' adventurous years that included white water rafting in Snake River Idaho, an African safari, South Dakota motorcycle rally, Ireland, Hawaii, Australia, scores of national horse shows and major horse racing events around the country

When anniversary dates of Barbara Jo's jockey career surface, media coverage requests her appearance or interviews. Barbara Jo welcomes the interest in her historic relevance for the sake of nostalgia but hardly lives in that past.

She stepped back into the limelight when it shines on women jockeys in the Lady Legends race during Preakness week at Pimlico. Barbara Jo rode in the sisterhood race for four years beginning when she was sixty years old.

Beyond the recognition of the ladies and festivities with good friends, the soiree raises funds for breast cancer. Barbara Jo's other charitable work includes fundraising for disabled jockeys at the Tampa jockey reunion.

She shares her unwavering perspective, "I feel blessed to do what I love with horses."

Barbara Jo's comfortable Classic Acres home was furnished in horse and hunting decor. Happy pictures of the couple, friends, horses, and dogs are displayed prominently. Their office features ribbons, trophies, and other items of achievement and honors. Barbara Jo's horses retire from a good life at Classic Acres and are laid to rest on a shady grassy hillside.

When the last batch of foals came to the Classic Acres barn, B.J. cared for them with the doting vitality of a twenty-year-old mother. Each horse and human on the property feels loved.

Tucked away inside the house is a trunk that belonged to Barbara Jo's mother, Maxine. It's filled with stacks of newspaper and magazine articles, racing reports, memorabilia and photographs all about her daughter.

Fond memories define a life well lived but the daily treasures are what matter the most. It delights B.J. when she stirs awake during the night and finds Gordie holding her hand. She loves a man who has always seen her beauty, her heart and her soul. Gordie tells her that he loves her every day.

Reminiscent of the last scene in, National Velvet, *the only way to come back is to go.* Barbara Jo has done the journey.

Barbara Jo and Gordie are now fully retired in Florida with a small barn of horses and a lifetime of incredible memories.

REFERENCES

FILMS/MOTION PICTURES

Wonke, A. (Director). 2015. Being AP (film). BBC Film

Osmond, L. (Director). 2015. Dark Horse (film). Darlow Smithson

Meehl, C. (Director). 2010. Buck (film). Cedar Creek

Orion, M. (Director). 2010. The Horse Boy (film). Zeitgeist Films

WORLDWIDE WEB

Wikipedia

NEWSPAPERS

Miami News, Miami Herald, Miami Beach Sun, St. Pete Times, Baltimore Sun, New York Times, New York Daily News New York Sunday News, New York Morning Telegraph, Louisville Courier Journal, El Paso Times, Decatur Herald

BOOKS

Bornstein, M. (2015) Last Chance Mustang

Carver, N. (2014) Making Tracks the Untold Story of Horse Racing Condron, B. (1997) The Dreamer's Dictionary

Cruise, D. (2023) Wild Horse Annie Velma Johnston

Farmer, S. (2006) Animal Spirit Guides

Gale Group, The, (2004) Notable Sports Figures

Hanley, L. (1973) The Lady Is a Jock

Hill, C. (2006) How to Think Like a Horse

Hillenbrand, L. (2001) Seabiscuit An American Legend

Hollander, P. (1972) American Women in Sports

Kohanov, L. (2001) The Tao of Equus

McEvoy, J. (2001) Women in Racing in Their Own Words

McEvoy, J. (2000) Great Horse Racing Mysteries

Meeder, K. (1996) Hope Rising

Mitchelle, E. (2022) Three Strides Before the Wire

Pagano, F.X. Sr. (2012) My Buddy King of the Hill

Scanlan, L. (2007) The Horse God Built Untold Story of Secretariat

Sewell, A., (1946) Black Beauty

Taylor, William T., 2024 December, Scientific American (article)

Made in the USA
Coppell, TX
16 January 2026

69393338R00095